The
Nation
City

The Nation City

Why Mayors Are Now Running the World

Rahm Emanuel

ALFRED A. KNOPF
New York
2020

THIS IS A BORZOI BOOK
PUBLISHED BY ALFRED A. KNOPF

www.aaknopf.com

Knopf, Borzoi Books, and the colophon are registered trademarks of Penguin Random House LLC.

Jacket photograph by Russell Kord/Alamy
Jacket design by Chip Kidd

Library of Congress Cataloging-in-Publication Data
Names: Emanuel, Rahm, 1959– author.
Title: The nation city : why mayors are now running the world / Rahm Emanuel.
Description: New York : Alfred A. Knopf, 2020. |
    Includes bibliographical references.
Identifiers: LCCN 2019024936 (print) | LCCN 2019024937 (ebook) |
    ISBN 9780525656388 (hardcover) | ISBN 9780525656395 (ebook)
Subjects: LCSH: Mayors—United States. | Municipal government—
    United States. | Municipal services—United States—Management. |
    Political leadership—United States. | Government accountability—
    United States. | United States—Politics and government—
    21st century.
Classification: LCC JS356 .E63 2020 (print) | LCC JS356 (ebook) |
    DDC 352.23/2160973—dc23
LC record available at https://lccn.loc.gov/2019024936
LC ebook record available at https://lccn.loc.gov/2019024937

Manufactured in the United States of America
First Edition

In memory of Dr. Benjamin Emanuel,
my father, my friend, my mentor

For Amy, Zachariah, Ilana, and Leah

I strongly believe being mayor is the public post in which you have the greatest opportunity to change people's lives for the better.

—EDUARDO PAES, former mayor of Rio de Janeiro

Contents

The
Nation
City

Introduction

On an early morning in the fall of 1917, Herman Smulevitz hurriedly kissed his mother and then slipped onto a ship docked at a port on the Black Sea. He was ten years old. He would never see his mother again.

World War I was nearing its end and Russia was in turmoil, in the midst of a revolution that would soon lead to a civil war. The country, and vast parts of eastern Europe, were swept up in what would become the third wave of devastating pogroms—the organized massacres of Jews that had been periodically ravaging this part of the world for more than a century. This last wave was the most savage of them all. Anti-Semitic mobs, stirred into a frenzy by the chaos in Russia, raped and pillaged and murdered Jews in the former Polish-Lithuanian lands within Russian borders, known as the Pale of Settlement, where Herman and his mother lived.

Herman's mother had come to the stark conclusion that the only chance of survival her son had was to flee to the United

States. She was most likely correct: There is no record of her existence after she told her son goodbye that day.

I am eternally grateful and indebted to her for her sacrifice and for the love she had for her son. Herman Smulevitz was my grandfather.

Herman boarded that boat by himself, a stowaway. He had with him only a few useless coins in his pockets and a note with the name of his father, who had abandoned his family and left for the U.S. after Herman was born, and the word "Indiana" written on it. Weeks later, Herman landed at Ellis Island in New York City, that great gateway of hope and renewed dreams for so many like him, and made his way to a small town in Indiana. There he somehow found his father's house. But when he arrived at the front door—unable to speak English, dirty, and probably wearing the same tattered clothes he'd had on since the day he left Russia—his new stepmother shut the door in his face, turning him away. With nowhere else to go, Herman traveled to Chicago, where he found an uncle who worked on Maxwell Street, a gateway neighborhood for immigrants on the Near West Side of the city. It was there that my grandfather began to seize his opportunity for a new life.

My grandfather's formal education ended in the fifth grade, but he sat at the kitchen table every morning before breakfast and forced himself to read newspapers and books, teaching himself to speak English and learning about the world. He started earning a wage as a young teen, jumping from one odd job to the next, sweeping floors or delivering goods on foot. He grew quickly and grandly, exiting his teenage years as a six-foot-three, 230-pound man. He began to box. He fought for prize money all over the Midwest, though he was denied the chance to fight for the bigger purses offered in the South because of his Jewish surname. He had huge hands, with fingers "like big Polish sausages," as my brother Ezekiel always described them. He later found work in lumberyards and steel mills. He butchered meat. He was a union man through and through, and would become a staunch Franklin Delano Roosevelt Democrat. His longest-serving job was as a deliveryman for Scandinavian Meat. He was charismatic and loud and profane, a big presence, and not just physically. My two brothers and I nicknamed him "Big Banger," which, when we said it, sounded like "Big Bangah." He was a tough, hard man, a true laborer, but also a people person. Sometimes he would take my brothers and me with him on his deliveries. He'd barge into a store and shake the hands and slap the backs of everyone he saw. He knew everyone's name, it seemed, and everyone knew his. Later in his life he would help build a community synagogue on Kedzie Avenue. He eventually moved to North Lawndale, on the old West Side of Chicago, then known as the "vest side" to his fellow eastern European Jews who lived there.

At a dance one night in Douglas Park in the mid-1920s, Herman met a woman named Sophie Lampert. She had her own remarkable immigration story, having only recently escaped from Moldova, a part of Romania, on a ship with her two sisters. Herman and Sophie eventually got married and had three daughters and two sons. One of those daughters was named Marsha. She is my mother.

Marsha became a radiologist technician at Mount Sinai Hospital in the North Lawndale community. There she met a man named Benjamin Emanuel, a pediatrician who worked at the hospital. His father, Ezekiel Auerbach, had been a pharmacist in Israel. When the family lived in Israel, Benjamin's brother, Manuel, was struck in the leg by a bullet while attending a protest in

Jerusalem in 1933. He died a few weeks later from an infection. Soon after, the Auerbachs changed their surname to Emanuel in his honor.

Benjamin and Marsha married and had three sons—Ezekiel (Zeke), and then me, and then Ariel (Ari)—and later adopted a daughter named Shoshana. We grew up in a series of different apartments in Chicago, starting in neighborhoods with low rents and a mix of immigrants, Jews and Catholics and poor whites who had migrated north from southern Appalachia. We fled one of those apartments—a crumbling flat with leaky faucets and peeling paint—because one night my mother found a rat sitting next to me in my crib. (We moved to Wilmette when I was in the fifth grade. I would return to the city—to Cornelia Avenue in Wrigleyville—after graduating from college in 1982.)

My father coupled his hospital job with a private practice, and he worked seventy hours a week seeing a range of patients, from those so poor that he provided them with free treatment to the sons and daughters of famous ballplayers on the Chicago Cubs. But he always made time for his kids. His favorite game to play with us was chess. He never took it easy on us, never let us win. He encouraged us to think three moves ahead and always to imagine our opponent's response to our potential moves.

My mother was an activist. She believed that it was our duty to fight for people who were suffering in this world. She was arrested numerous times while protesting. She stood in the crowd at the Mall in Washington, D.C., and watched Martin Luther King, Jr., deliver his "I have a dream" speech. She marched in protests with her three toddler sons in tow, and always took us along to the polling station to watch her vote. She took us to hear King speak in Chicago in 1966. She helped organize a local chapter of the Congress of Racial Equality. Our landlord kicked our family out of an apartment on West Buena Avenue because he didn't like the mixed-race gatherings my mother hosted there.

I know it might be hard to believe now, but I grew up as a quiet, attentive child. My mother and brothers tell me that I didn't speak much when we were gathered together, but merely observed. That changed after an incident when I was seventeen. I sliced the middle finger on my right hand while working one day at my job at an Arby's. The finger—and my hand and arm—eventually became infected, and I spent seven weeks in the hospital. The doctors were able to save my hand and arm, but they were forced to remove half of my middle finger. I don't remember much after the surgery, but Zeke told me that when the doctor unwrapped my hand for the first time, I flipped everyone the bird and then declared that I would have to do it twice now for the desired effect. Something changed in me after that accident. A quiet, introverted kid suddenly became transformed into a garrulous teen full of energy and a fierce and focused desire to succeed.

———

While we were growing up, the city of Chicago was our playground. There were movie theaters, libraries, museums, a zoo, parks, and a mass transit system that made it possible to get to all of those places. There were people of all different backgrounds and races and religious beliefs who had one thing in common: a profound yearning to improve their lot in life. The city had its hazards, too. There was poverty and crime. There were dark alleys that we avoided. My brothers and I were more than once taunted for being Jewish. The city shaped us. It held all of the promise and all of the peril in the world.

At the center of everything was Big Bangah. By the time he

and Sophie were in their late forties, they'd scraped together enough money to move from North Lawndale to Albany Park, on the Northwest Side of Chicago. Their new neighborhood wasn't materially much nicer or further up the socioeconomic ladder than their old one, but it was a solid blue-collar area (as it is today), and it did signify to Big Bangah that he had scratched and clawed his way firmly into the lower middle class. My grandparents were over the moon about the move, believing they had made it. (My father's private medical practice had served Albany Park, my uncle was a cop there, and I would wind up representing the neighborhood in my first years in the U.S. Congress. The joke in our family was that we had traveled many miles but we had never gotten very far.)

Every Sunday, with no exceptions or excuses tolerated, we all went to Big Bangah and Sophie's for dinner on the third floor of a three-flat, where we were joined by my aunt Shirley and her six kids and two of my uncles. These dinners were not sedate affairs. There was chaos everywhere, with kids running around and political arguments at the table that ended in shouting matches. There was no peace. There was no quiet. But we always entered the house as a family, and then, after all the battles and bickering, we left that same way, sent off with kisses from Sophie and a huge bear hug from Big Bangah. All to be repeated the following Sunday.

Big Bangah never explicitly told us what he expected from us in our lives, but it was implicit in everything he said and did, and we all heard it, loud and clear. And if we ever needed an actual physical reminder, all we had to do was look at a framed piece that hung on my parents' family room wall. Within it was the purse that Sophie had had with her when she arrived in America. Sticking out of the purse were the immigration papers that she and her two sisters had had with them then. The most haunting aspect of the piece, though, was the black-and-white photos surrounding the purse—pictures of my mother's and father's families, of the aunts and uncles and cousins whom we never got to meet because they never got out of eastern Europe and presumably succumbed to either the pogroms or, later, the Holocaust.

The contents of those photos mesmerized my brothers and me. The message conveyed by them—and by the life and deeds of our grandparents—was simple: *We sacrificed and struggled and left behind family that we never saw again. That sacrifice will not be dismissed. You are going to work hard to get an education. How dare you get a B on your report card? You are going to make something of yourself.*

Big Bangah and Sophie eventually moved into our home for a while, and we got to feel and witness this message in a closer and more powerful way. Though Big Bangah was retired by that time, he rose at 4:30 a.m. out of habit, to read newspapers and books at the kitchen table and continue his self-education, sitting there in a tank top, boxers, knee-high socks, and slippers. There was no ambiguity when it came to the meaning of his life. Big Bangah had worked his ass off in pursuit of his big dream: that his children and grandchildren would be provided with an education and the opportunities for better lives than he'd had.

We internalized his dream. There is a reason that Zeke is a leading oncologist and bioethicist and that Ari runs one of the most significant talent agencies in the world and that Shoshana has overcome her physical disabilities to lead a happy and productive life.

I took Big Bangah's dream, sprinkled in my father's work ethic and my mother's activism and their shared desire to help those who were suffering and in need, and entered the world of politics. I joined my first campaign in 1980, working for David Robinson in his ultimately unsuccessful bid for the U.S. House of Representatives. Two years later, after finishing college at Sarah Lawrence, I joined the very successful campaign of U.S. Senator Paul Simon. I got a master's degree in speech and communications at Northwestern and then became first the regional director and then the political director of the Democratic Congressional Campaign Committee (DCCC). In 1991, I joined Bill Clinton's campaign for the U.S. presidency and then his administration, where I would become the senior adviser. In the midst of all of this, I found and married Amy and we had three great children, creating a family that is the love of my life. I took a two-year break from politics to work in finance and then ran for the U.S. House of Representatives. I won four consecutive terms as the representative of Illinois's fifth congressional district and ended up running the DCCC and chairing the House Democratic Caucus. And just as I had won my fourth term and positioned myself to become perhaps the first Jewish Speaker of the House, I answered the call of then President-elect Barack Obama and became his chief of staff at the beginning of his first term in 2008.

In 2010, I resigned from that position. I did so because I realized that I had a chance to go after something I felt I was born to do, something that would bring Big Bangah's story—my family's story—full circle. I left one of the most powerful positions in our federal government to pursue a job that in many ways is more impactful, and in every way is more satisfying: the mayoralty of my hometown, Chicago.

My brothers, chasing their ambitions, had both left Chicago—Zeke for Europe and then the East Coast, Ari for New York City and then Los Angeles. I had left Chicago, too, for a bit, to go to college and then to work for both the Clinton and the Obama administrations. But the city had never left me. I loved its reality, its brawn, its beauty, its people, its potential, its promise. I knew at this point, from my experiences, that something was deeply broken in our federal government. It was dysfunctional, and only getting worse with each ensuing year. Because of packed courts, gerrymandering, and the influence of special interests, it was also no longer a progressive entity, no longer the deliverer of programs and policies that actually *helped* the people who needed it. I realized that cities were the last places where progressive politics existed. This was not something to fear; it was something to embrace. Chicago and all of our cities here in the United States, as well as those abroad, offered a pathway out of the dysfunction of our national governments and into a more progressive future. And I wanted to play a role in shaping that future.

And in 2011—exactly ninety-four years after Big Bangah arrived on the shores of Lake Michigan, penniless and tattered but ready to seize his opportunity—I became the forty-fourth mayor of the city of Chicago. This is our family's version of the American Dream, a dream made possible by our great city.

Chicago is no different from any city in the world: It's always been a place of opportunity. And those opportunities that our cities around the globe provide have never been more apparent— or more important—than they are now.

The opportunities in our cities are facilitated now by our mayors, who run the only governments left in the world that are immediate, intimate, and impactful. Just when the federal government is distant, the local government is intimate. Just when the federal government is dysfunctional, the local government is impactful. Just when the federal government is indifferent, the local government is immediate. Local governments are politically stable when our national governments are anything but. Pressing questions are being asked today of our national governments by the citizens of the world. The answers to those questions are found in cities and with their mayors.

Mayors are faced with the task of making their cities places where people can live, work, and play. At the most basic level, mayors have to do the essential tasks that keep a city going on a day-to-day basis. They have to get the garbage picked up, the snow plowed, and the potholes filled. They must balance the budget.

But they also have the bigger issues to deal with. The educational system must be a good, innovative, and fair one. There must be cultural events and venues, playgrounds, parks and other green spaces, libraries, and effective modes of public transportation. There must be an appreciation of and respect for diversity. There must be room to welcome immigrants. There must be wisdom and forethought when it comes to the issue of climate change.

Mayors and cities fall short on some of these issues. They are still works in progress. But our local governments come closer to solving them than national governments do, by a long shot.

All of our world's challenges—the perils—are found in cities. But so are all of the ideas, energy, willpower, and resources—the promises—needed to confront those challenges. National governments are not keeping up with the times. Those come now from the local level, where citizens have the ability to play a real role in governance. In cities they have a voice, and it is heard. Mayors listen and learn and lead. Mayors are accountable—

citizens can tell them what they think about their performance in an immediate and intimate sense. We have cups of coffee together. We commute to work together. We worship together. We celebrate together. We grieve together. Our local governments and cities provide a place to satisfy our craving for a sense of community and our yearning to belong and be a part of something that is meaningful and bigger than ourselves. That intimacy should not be overlooked. The disinformation and the conspiracy theories that flood social media are almost all about national politics and politicians and not about local ones. There's a reason for that: We know each other too well to fall for it.

All mayors make mistakes—I made my share during my two terms in Chicago. But good mayors never shy away from addressing issues head-on. And this is how progress is made.

Mayors have great power now because of the proximity of the perils and the promises found in their cities, and because of the immediacy, the intimacy, the impactfulness of the governments they run.

With that power comes a great responsibility.

———

I still marvel at the fact that the grandson and the son of immigrants could be a key adviser to two presidents, walk the halls of Congress as a member and a leader, and be elected mayor of the city Herman and Sophie made our home.

As mayor, I concluded that a major shift was happening. The national government was in retreat and cities were emerging as the new power centers filling the void. About a hundred cities around the world drive the economic, cultural, and intellectual energy of our planet today. And that will only grow in the years ahead.

As national governments teeter, local governments offer political stability. On the economic front, cities are more dynamic. In almost all things, cities act with a greater sense of urgency. Cities and mayors have to act *now*. There is no sign hanging on the door that says GONE FISHING FOR THE SUMMER.

To meet their new challenges and respond to the void left by national governments, two new phenomena are emerging. First, ideas and answers move horizontally, not vertically. No one expects anything significant from Washington, Brussels, or London—so we share, copy, and plagiarize all the time.

Second, the old federal/local partnership has for all practical purposes ceased to exist. It has been replaced by a new paradigm: a partnership led by universities, community groups, nonprofits, the private sector, and local government.

This book is an attempt to help us all recognize what is happening in politics today—taking lessons from Chicago's City Hall, Capitol Hill, and the West Wing—and be cognizant of the promise and peril of the current moment.

Put on your helmet and fasten your seatbelt: It's a wild ride!

ONE

An Education

To Big Bangah, education was everything. Not for him personally, of course. For all intents and purposes, he had had no real formal education. But for his kids and grandkids, he prioritized a good education as the gateway to greater opportunity. It was the centerpiece of his life.

And here's where the great responsibility part for mayors comes into play. I embraced Big Bangah's mindset with my whole heart. While attending Sarah Lawrence, I considered early childhood education as a career. Education reform—providing equal opportunities for every child in my city—was central to my tenure as the mayor of Chicago. It was by far the single most important thing I did. That's because education is the key to putting us on the path to solving what is perhaps the most pressing issue in the United States and maybe even the world today. It's the issue in which mayors stand on the front line.

That issue is income inequality.

There are a lot of different ways to begin to address and attack that problem, from taxes to minimum wage to housing. But the single most important tool we have to start to try to narrow the income and opportunity gap is education.

The fight for providing a good education for *all* of our children gets to the core of the tension in this book, the heart of the problem we now face as a country—and a world—and the heart of the solution. Put simply, the federal government in the U.S. has almost completely walked away from its duty to take care of the education of the country's children. It wasn't always this way. Back in the progressive era of the 1960s, the federal government actually led the way. In 1965, as part of the Great Society, President Lyndon Johnson created Head Start, an enormously important federal program that funded local early education projects. It was a boon for local governments in dire circumstances and for the families that depended on it.

But that era is now over. Fast-forward fifty years from the founding of Head Start. As you'll see in a moment, President Obama tried to do something similar, tried to enact a policy that would have changed the trajectories of the lives of millions of children in a very positive way. But by this time in our nation's history, it had become nearly impossible for even the best ideas to initiate and spread from the federal level. President Obama's policy was blocked, of course, held back by a federal government that had become sclerotic, partisan, and broken. To his credit, President Obama didn't give up on our nation's children. He pivoted away from his own federal government and sought help from another group of politicians, pleading with them to take his idea and run with it. He did this because he believed, correctly, that these politicians were the only ones today who could get it done. Fifty years earlier, mayors had to rely on the federal government for resources and reinvention; now President Obama, in the name of the federal government, needed mayors to help him make actionable change.

And we did just that and more. Nothing better exemplifies the transformation of our federal/local government dichotomy.

———

Early on in his second term, President Obama began to work on what he believed would be a signature achievement of his presidency. He wanted the federal government to implement and fund a program in which all three- and four-year-olds in the country would be guaranteed schooling. The concept is popularly known as universal pre-K.

Obama knew how high the stakes were, and he had done his research on young children and education. There was a lot of it, dating back to the 1960s. The Perry Preschool Project—which provided high-level preschool education to disadvantaged African American children from 1962 to 1967—later demonstrated that by age forty, those who had attended preschool were less likely to have committed a crime and more likely to have a job than those who had not gone to preschool. More recently, the Social Genome Project, a joint effort of the Brookings Institution, the Urban Institute, and Child Trends, showed that preschool could change the lives of low-income children: It makes them more ready for school, and boosts their cognitive and behavioral outcomes to nearly that of their high-income peers. The research of the economist and Nobel Memorial Prize winner James Heckman established that early childhood education is the most effective recipe for better health, productivity, and success in school and in the individual's life, and reduces deficits and makes for a stronger economy for society at large.

There was a time when President Obama's smart and reasonable idea would have had a good chance of becoming law. Education in the U.S. has an interesting history and has traveled a looping path. The great transformation of our country's education system began in the late nineteenth century, and the state and federal governments didn't lead it. Local governments were largely responsible for building and funding the high school system, and the states did the same for the community college system that we have today. And because of that, "we went from a country that in 1890 had 10 percent of its young people getting a secondary education to a country that by 1940 had 90 percent of its young people getting a secondary education," says Philip Zelikow, a diplomat, author, and professor of history at the University of Virginia. "We would enter World War II with the most educated workforce in the entire world, and that turned out to be important." After the war, the federal government adopted many of the best education ideas and spread them far and wide. The GI Bill would end up being one of the most significant national education policies ever enacted. The National Defense Education Act, passed on the heels of Russia's launch of Sputnik, funded scientific research. The ACT test was created. The Elementary and Secondary School Act and Higher Education Act were passed in 1965.

And then the ideas and programs implemented from the federal level began to slow. In the 1980s, President Ronald Reagan threatened to eliminate the Department of Education, which President Jimmy Carter had created. Though Reagan didn't succeed, the message was out there: The federal government should have no role in education. Excessive partisanship eventually made Reagan's dream a reality.

And once again ideas and innovations in education have been left to our mayors and local governments.

———

President Obama worked hard to craft and pass a universal pre-K bill that would transform millions of young lives. But to his endless frustration, the idea never really got off the ground. He'd had some success with education initiatives. In fact, in his first term—with a Democratic Congress, of course—he passed Race to the Top, a $4.35 billion federal government grant-making program designed to spur innovation in K-12 education. But by 2014 the Republicans controlled Congress, and his best ideas went nowhere. His pre-K initiative was one of the casualties of partisanship, held up by an obstruction-bound Republican Congress that didn't give it a chance. So President Obama did something that I think was very telling. He turned to the government officials who actually could get things like this done: mayors. Just like when Congress stifled his attempt to increase the federal minimum wage, he turned to mayors across the country to get it done. In early 2015, with the chances of passage of his universal pre-K bill pretty much dead, President Obama convened two hundred mayors and mayors-elect from across the nation. During that meeting he implored those men and women to do in their respective cities what he and the federal government could not do for the country as a whole.

The mayors responded. New York City mayor Bill de Blasio convinced his state to fund universal pre-K for his city, in what was the finest moment of his tenure. The program currently enrolls 70,000 kids. Mayor Jim Kenney of Philadelphia has essentially created a universal pre-K program in his city, funded by taxes on sugary drinks. Jenny Durkan in Seattle, Marty Walsh in Boston, Nan Whaley in Dayton, and former mayor Julián Castro in San Antonio have put their cities on the path to providing the service. A partial list of other cities working on universal pre-K plans includes Charlotte, Cleveland, Columbus, Denver, Fort Worth, Jacksonville, Los Angeles, Nashville, Phoenix, Salt Lake City, and San Francisco.

And in Chicago? The fight for equitable school funding from the state started more than fifty years ago, under then-mayor Richard J. Daley. That battle was still raging when I took over as mayor. Illinois was ranked dead last when it came to equitable funding for the education of disadvantaged children. I decided that I would try to end it once and for all.

However, before I could start with pre-K, I had to address the kindergarten divide. In my first term, I started with a simple goal. Chicago at the time was the only major city in the country that did not have full-day universal kindergarten. In 2011, just over half of the city's kids had full-day kindergarten. We also had the shortest school day and the shortest school year in the country. I made it my mission in the first contract negotiations of 2012 to get full-day kindergarten for every child and a full school day and a full school year for every child in Chicago. And that is what we accomplished. By 2013 all of the kids had full-day kindergarten. Then it was time to focus on full-day universal pre-K.

Having accomplished full-day kindergarten for every child, I, with my close friend and adviser Michael Sacks and senior staff led by Mike Rendina, developed a simple strategy to achieve full-day universal pre-K: Instead of having to beg the state for funding, we would take the fight to, and put the onus on, the state. As the mayor of Chicago, I was in charge of the city's 600-plus public schools, and thus in charge of the budget. After some brainstorming with my staff, we realized that we could rewrite the state's education funding formula to free up resources for universal full-day pre-K. We did just that, and then we lobbied the state legislature hard and soon had the votes to get it passed. The only thing standing in our way was the Republican governor of the state, who called the bill a "bailout for Chicago," as every Republican governor had done for the last fifty years. We decided to put the squeeze on him. We sent him the bill that included the new funding formula a week before the opening of all Illinois schools. That way, had he vetoed it, he would have owned the shutdown of every public school in the state, not just Chicago's schools. As you may have guessed, he decided to sign the bill, and Chicago received the additional $45 million windfall for pre-K, which started in the 2017–18 school year. By 2021 the program will be fully funded (at $175 million), and Chicago will have full-day pre-K for all of its students. As a bonus, the new funding formula led the credit agencies to upgrade the schools' ratings.

This was no small matter. Governor Bruce Rauner and I battled for the better part of two years to rewrite the school funding formula. He was determined to drive Chicago public schools into bankruptcy. In fact, when the schools were in the market on a bond issuance, he tried to undermine the financing. Poor children would have been the victims of his ideological objective: breaking the teachers' union. Our fight became personal and acrimonious. We started as good friends, but that is not how our relationship ended. By forcing him to sign the legislation, we ended a fifty-year battle between Chicago and Illinois.

Between his veto threat and his signature, we were able to add $400-plus million to the funding for Chicago schools. Rather than bankruptcy, Chicago public schools were upgraded by the rating agencies, all families received full-day pre-K for their children, and our teachers had their pensions secured. Not bad for a day's work.

———

As I've said, when I came into office in 2011, Chicago public schools had the shortest school day and year in the nation. Teachers were literally being forced to choose between reading and recess and between math and music. Those are no-win choices in my mind. There needs to be time for all of it (yes, even recess; I'm a firm believer that recess is about much more than just running around). And it drove me absolutely crazy that, based on school hours, kids in Houston were getting *three years* more education from kindergarten to twelfth grade than our students were in Chicago. Nearly 80 percent of our 381,000 public school kids are at the poverty line or below, and there was no way that cycle of poverty had a chance of being broken with the shortest school day and year in the country.

Richard M. Daley had tried to add time to the school day but had been stymied by the leadership of the teachers' union. They wanted much more pay for even the slightest increase in schooling time. In the 2003 and 2007 contracts they indeed got more pay—4 percent a year for a decade—but no additional time was added to the school day. My predecessor's biggest fear—and the union's biggest weapon—was the threat of a strike.

So I decided we would do whatever it took to make a longer school day and year happen. If that meant enduring a strike, so be it. I was willing to take the political pain. And when we brought up the idea of adding more time to the school day, the union did indeed threaten to strike.

We secured the reform, adding an extra hour and fifteen minutes to the school day. We also added nearly two full weeks to the school year and rewrote the outdated evaluations used to keep the city's educators (the teachers and principals) accountable. We made a fair deal: Teachers received a pay raise and children received the added and necessary time in class.

Yes, the teachers did strike. It was a painful seven days, of course. Every morning I woke up to three hundred of my closest friends outside my house yelling my name and telling me I sucked. My kids endured protests at their schools from union representatives. One morning, after my daily workout, I stood at the door, about to embark on the thirty-foot walk to the car to go to City Hall, a walk that felt more like thirty miles. I could hear the chants on the other side of my door. Amy approached me to say goodbye and then stopped suddenly. "I've seen you through an impeachment, through health-care reform, an auto bailout, a balanced budget act, and an assault-weapons ban," she said. "But I have to be honest, you've never seemed calmer." Just then we heard a loud "Rahm sucks!" from outside. "Amy," I replied, "I've never felt more right about what I'm doing. I owe it to the parents. Screw this BS about saying one thing in the campaign and another thing after you get elected. More than that, I owe Chicago's kids a chance." As I kissed Amy goodbye, she opened the door and stepped to the side as the sounds of the chants blew through the house.

During the strike, I thought a lot about one more key issue: the autonomy of principals. The question was whether individual principals would have the ability to hire teachers of their own choosing or whether, as the union preferred, principals would have to select from a limited pool that was functionally chosen and maintained by the union.

Mahalia Ann Hines, a former Chicago school principal (who happens to be the artist Common's mother; I had appointed her to the school board), pulled me aside one day before a press conference. Hines, who holds a doctorate from the University of Illinois, had spent fifteen years as a principal, at grade levels from elementary through high school. If we were going to make lasting improvements to Chicago's schools, she argued, principals needed flexibility. Without it, they would not be able to create an effective team and establish the right culture in their schools. And, at least as important, principals needed the leverage to coach teachers struggling to help their pupils succeed. "We can't undercut the principals," she said. "Parents and teachers are vital, of course, but the principals are the keys." I agreed with her. So I added principal autonomy to my demands.

The strike dragged on for two additional days because of principal autonomy. After its conclusion, I decided to go all in on principal-centered reform. We raised principals' salaries, particularly for those working in challenging schools. We collaborated with Northwestern University to improve professional development for principals and established a new program explicitly designed to recruit and train new school leaders. We also gave the best-performing principals additional autonomy by establishing a system of independent public schools, subject to less oversight from the central office, which gave them greater ability to compete with charter schools. All vital and necessary steps to improve our schools. None of it was easy, but it was accomplished. At all times I appointed one, if not two, principals to the school board. Presently, two great principals, Dr. Janice Jackson and LaTanya McDade, are leading Chicago public schools.

Here's the upshot: People remember the strike but also appreciate the extra two and a half years of classroom time that has been added to our students' kindergarten through twelfth-grade years, the universal kindergarten, the updated evaluations, the growing excellence of our principals and schools.

Here are a few other things that came about because of the reforms:

- High school graduation rate grew from 56.9% to 78.9%
- Freshmen on track to graduate grew from 69% to 89.4%
- Students who read at or above national levels grew from 45.6% to 61.8%
- Students who mastered math at or above national levels grew from 45.1% to 56.7%
- Among the one hundred largest school districts in the country, Chicago has the highest growth rate between third and eighth grade
- Even though we're an urban school system, our children now match the national averages in college and community college enrollment. Also, we have the lowest dropout rate ever recorded: 6%

The "Rahm sucks!" protesters stopped showing up in front of my house. But don't worry, they were replaced soon enough by other protesters upset about housing, the minimum wage, and any other set of issues I tried to tackle.

A little more than a year after getting the longer school day and year, we took one more step: We shuttered forty-nine failing schools in 2013. We also implemented an accountability system that resulted in closing numerous charter schools in later years. The debate in Chicago was not between neighborhood and charter schools but between quality versus mediocrity. Closing one school, let alone forty-nine, is never a popular thing to do, and I took some serious flak for it. But in this case we had to. Yes, it potentially stressed the rest of the school system. But these concerns were overridden by the fact that these schools were consistently failing, and the students who attended them were trapped in that failure, with no prospect for improvement.

As a part of all this, we've also enhanced our investments in our childrens' lives outside of the classroom (where kids spend 80 percent of their time), focusing on extra learning. We've opened up libraries in some nontraditional spaces (we call this "co-locating"), including ones in three new public housing facilities in the city—beautiful buildings designed by Skidmore, Owings & Merrill (why shouldn't public housing be beautiful, too?). When we were looking to fund this idea, we noticed a line item within the Chicago Housing Authority budget regulations that was called "community investments." We researched it and discovered that libraries qualify. *The New York Times* has cited these co-located libraries as "striking new civic architecture," an advertisement for the city, and a source of community pride. Co-location was also just plain good urban planning. In fact, we convinced President Obama to locate a neighborhood library inside his new presidential library in Hyde Park.

These libraries function as resource centers and quiet spaces where kids can study. And within those new libraries and all of the other seventy-nine in the city, we've provided free tutoring in every subject for three hours after every school day. The libraries also offer free online tutoring in any subject, in both English and Spanish, the only system to provide such a service. No longer will the well-off be the only people who can access tutoring for their children. This new program has been a huge success: So far we've had more than 120,000 tutoring sessions within our libraries.

In the summer, when the dreaded academic "slide" occurs with many children, we've intervened with a program called Rahm's Readers. If any child reads at least three books over the summer, he or she receives a free backpack full of books as a reward. This program also takes place in our libraries, which, I have to say, I am very proud of. Our neighborhood library system has been recognized as the best in the country. Libraries are such an integral part of our community, not only a place for schoolkids and their learning but one of the few places left where people of all different incomes, races, religions, and backgrounds come together and share experiences. (They also have citizenship centers where the undocumented can get information on immigration and study for citizenship exams.)

To top it all off, we grew the number of summer jobs for high schoolers to 33,000, up from 14,500 when I became mayor. We have about 115,000 kids in after-school programs, dramatically more than when we began. We stepped in where the federal government had stepped away. With money drying up, the federal government's once-robust summer jobs program in Chicago, like those in other cities, has dwindled to a minimal amount.

Through all the changes, disagreements, and fights in the early years, I and Karen Lewis, the head of the teachers' union, eventually developed a strong working relationship and mutual respect. And, boy, were there fights. During the 2015 contract negotiations, she partnered with me in strengthening the teachers' pensions with reforms. In 1983, Mayor Harold Washington had agreed to allow teachers to pay only 2 percent toward their pensions. In 2015, Karen and I worked together to have all new teachers pay their full portion of 9 percent. This enabled the city to make the state finally pay *their* portion ($215 million, part of the new funding formula). Today, Chicago teachers' pensions are some of the better-funded in the state, which may not be saying much, but it's something. Let me just say, Karen is a worthy adversary and a worthy partner. I prefer partner.

———

Income and opportunity inequality is our national challenge. It is much worse in the United States than it is in other countries, and the gap between the haves and have-nots has been getting wider over the last four decades. The numbers are staggering. According to Bruce Katz and Jeremy Nowak, in their indispensable book, *The New Localism*: "Today, the top ten percent of U.S. earners average about nine times the income of the bottom ninety percent of earners. In terms of wealth, the top ten percent of Americans have about $5 trillion in net worth, while the bottom half has about $1 trillion."

A huge related problem is that there is very little economic mobility these days. The Social Genome Project study showed that kids born in the bottom income quintile have, at best, a 30 percent chance of reaching the middle class during their lifetime. A huge swath of our population is now being left behind.

Cities are living this divide every day. You can walk thirty minutes from any central business district and find significant disparities in wealth. This is part of the peril found in cities. But we're all in this together. Whenever I talk to Chicago business groups, I emphasize this point. They may not realize it, but they have a serious, vested interest in this issue. I tell them that if we don't figure out how to get more people into the winner's circle, Chicago will stop being a global city on the move. Income inequality and access to opportunity are issues that affect everyone.

In my opinion, the number-one job and priority of all mayors is to establish a level set for all of the citizens of their city. Not everyone will achieve success if you do that, of course. But at the very least everyone will be provided with the opportunity to do so.

Universal full-day pre-K is a great start. Universal full-day kindergarten, longer school days and years, tutoring, after-school programs, and summer reading and jobs are all important rungs on the education development ladder. But in order to truly take care of our children—and help establish that level set—we need to do more. During the industrial age, a high school diploma was the gateway to the American Dream. In the digital age, this is no longer the case. In order to give our kids a real chance these days, we must provide them with a full education, from pre-K through college.

Though our programs are not yet perfect and still have some kinks to work out, that's precisely what we've done in Chicago. Chicago is one of the first cities in America to redesign education from a K–12 model to a pre-K–college model.

And this is part of the promise.

———

Early on in my first term as mayor, my staff, led by policy chief David Spielfogel and his deputy, Michael Negron, began sending me memos with ideas. (I've made my policy people and department heads write weekly reports going back to my days in the Clinton administration.) I always looked forward to reading these memos. Many of the ideas were immensely practical. Others were the type of blue-sky thinking that gets you excited and stretches your imagination, despite its probable (or obvious) lack of practicality. But most of the ideas were somewhere in between these two poles: They were big ideas that, under the right circumstances and with some serious hustle and work, could possibly be accomplished.

In 2013, David and Michael sent me a memo that contained some ideas about education. By this juncture we had already lengthened the school day and school year, created universal full-day kindergarten, put universal full-day pre-K on track, and begun the process of converting our high schools to precollege educational institutions. David and Michael thought we could do more, something that encompassed the entire school life of our city's children. Along with the pre-K, elementary, middle, and high schools, the mayor in Chicago is in charge of the city's huge community college system, which encompasses seven colleges, numerous satellite sites, and more than 80,000 students. David, Michael, and I wondered if there might be something there, some sort of permanent stitching that we could do to make these disparate entities part of a greater whole.

I asked David and Michael to dig in deeper. The two of them started to pick the brains of all the smart people they knew, both in and out of the education world. At one point Bechara Choucair, our health commissioner, sent them an email. It read: "You guys see what they're doing in Tennessee?"

In early 2014 the Tennessee governor, Bill Haslam, a Republican and former businessman (and someone with some refreshingly bipartisan progressive ideas), had announced a plan for something he called the "Tennessee Promise," which guaranteed a free community college education for all graduating public school seniors. David and Michael researched the program and then showed me what they'd found and suggested that we just might be able to pull off something like this. "Let's do it," I said.

It happened to be a perfect fit for the reforms that were already under way. It complemented the ongoing renaissance of our high schools. It opened up a priceless opportunity to a whole group of deserving students. And it merged nicely with the reinvention of Chicago's community colleges, which had been a campaign pledge of mine in 2011.

With our community colleges, we had followed the German model. We repurposed every one of them so that each school focused on one of the seven top job-producing industries in the city: health care, transportation distribution and logistics, professional services, hospitality, advanced manufacturing, information technology, and social services. Some 150 local businesses in the city came in and helped make the curricula relevant. The reformation had a dramatic effect. Our community colleges had the worst graduation rate in the country when I took office (7 percent). Within two years they had one of the most improved graduation rates in the United States. Community college graduates were going into careers and not just jobs.

Our new idea would help propel those graduation rates even higher . . . and would help us with our larger mission: to ensure a great education for our children, from pre-K through college, and to deal with the diploma divide challenging our city. Kindergarten through twelfth grade is totally insufficient in today's economy. We all need to move toward a pre-K-to-college model, and a number of mayors on their own are pushing this new model.

One of our first calls was to Cheryl Hyman, who was then the chancellor of Chicago's community colleges. She loved the free community college idea. Her primary concern, though, was the cost to the community colleges, which would work out to around $4,000 per student.

That led us to our next internal discussion: What should be

the cutoff grade-point average to qualify for what amounted to a free scholarship? Or should we have one at all? We mulled over a 2.0 or 3.0 or 3.5 cutoff average. We took a look at what it would be like to have no cutoff.

The latter idea—to provide to everyone regardless of qualifications—is the *only* way to go about providing free college education in some circles of the Democratic Party. When we took a good hard look at that, I ended up disagreeing with that notion. For one, it would be impossible for us to pay for it. We were not receiving any federal or state help to fund it. We had to do it on our own. The city had already been spending $40 million a year in remedial education in the community colleges because of unprepared students. No cutoff would have exacerbated that problem, forcing the community colleges to hire scads of new teachers to teach students who weren't prepared for college, which would cost money and clog up the system. It would be unfair to send them very unprepared students and drain their already thinly stretched resources. Sending the community colleges above-average students would sweeten the deal: The community colleges would have eager, college-ready students who would make their schools stronger. And if we got better students, it would mean we wouldn't have to do much remedial teaching, and we would be incentivizing success rather than buying insurance on failure.

The second reason that the lack of a cutoff was not a feasible idea had to do with the buy-in of all the entities involved. They all had to bear some responsibility. The community colleges would provide free tuition, but the parents and kids had to have some skin in the game. I don't think it's ever practical to provide something for nothing. And I think this is a larger point when it comes to progressives. We have to be careful not to become the political entity that promises something for nothing. Yes, we want rights and we want programs that help people. But we must also have responsibilities that ensure those rights.

So we landed on a cutoff of a 3.0 (or B) average. It made the most economic and social sense. To add to this, we offered those who qualified for the program free books and free public transportation. We also devised a more focused high school curriculum, with more advanced-placement classes and dual-enrollment programs that partnered the community colleges with the high schools and better prepared those students for community college and beyond. Our dual-enrollment and dual-credit programs have flourished, going from 300 students enrolled in them to 5,000 now. Reinventing high school makes for a better college experience: In 2019 nearly half (49.9 percent) of our high school graduates had college or career credits when they graduated. (We also made sure *everyone* had a plan for life after high school. As of the 2019–20 school year, every high school student will have to provide a letter of acceptance from a community college, a four-year institution, the military, a trade school, or a job in order to receive their diploma.)

Now our Chicago public school students were all guaranteed an opportunity to get fourteen years of education—that's an extra four years of education added on since 2011—for the total cost of zero dollars.

Well, almost all the kids. There was some talk early on among my staff about the potential problems of including undocumented immigrant children in the program. (A local education publication estimated that they made up one third of the public school population.) The worry was about fraud and keeping track of the kids. But I was adamant on this point: We would include Dreamers in this program. It's who we are as a city, and

Chicago is also the city that my grandfather Big Bangah came to as an immigrant; it welcomed him, his children, and his grandchildren. And that was that.

The program, which officially began in October 2014, was called the Chicago Star Scholarship. It immediately energized the entire school system. As of 2019, we've had 6,500 Star Scholars.

Later in 2014 we embarked on an even bigger and more ambitious plan.

———

Around that time I read an article about the aftermath of the Great Recession. The article had some startling statistics within it. The rate of unemployment during the worst of the recession reached 11 percent. But it was the next fact that really grabbed my attention: Only 4.6 percent of those unemployed had a four-year college degree. In other words, having a four-year college degree was the best way to get—and keep—a job, even during the worst of times. (The unemployment rate for those with some college today is 3.5 percent; for those with at least a bachelor's degree, it's 2.1 percent.) And it's not just about jobs. It's about life and death. According to a study done by the Alliance for Excellent Education, people in the United States with fewer than twelve years of schooling have a death rate that is 2.5 times higher than those who complete thirteen years or more.

There are, of course, larger national—and even global—economic factors that are put upon us all and that we have to work within. The Great Recession is one of the latest and most profound examples. It made the job of being a mayor more difficult. But it also made the job more important, as it left our national government even more paralyzed.

I had that in mind when I got a call from the chancellor of the

University of Illinois at Chicago (UIC), Michael Amiridis. We later met in my office and I walked him through the Star program, describing the incredible opportunity that participating kids would now have.

Amiridis loved the program. "We can and should do more," he said in his thick Greek accent. "I want those kids in my university." UIC, like DePaul and Loyola, is a gateway for second-generation immigrants. He offered a new idea: If those Star Scholars maintained that B average during their two years in community college, he would offer them their remaining two years in college at his university for just $5,000 total. The more I thought about it, the more I believed that was not only an achievable goal but also an utterly necessary one. He didn't have to ask twice.

Then I thought, If UIC can do this, why can't the other Chicago-area universities do it, too? So I did what all politicians worth a bucket of warm spit do and held a big, loud press conference to announce UIC's involvement in the Star program. And right after that press conference I began to reach out to the other university presidents and told them, "Hey, UIC just did this. This is really important for the city and I want you in." I didn't have to twist any arms. I just showed them some of the infamous Rahm love. After the first sale, the next ones are always easier.

By late 2015 eleven more universities had become Star partners (we called this part of the program "Star Plus"), including the University of Chicago and DePaul. In 2016 Northwestern University joined our ranks. And in 2017 five more universities came onboard. By 2018 we had every university and college in the city and beyond (including the University of Illinois and three historic all-black colleges) signed on. All but one of them offered two years of college education for qualified Star Scholars for a significant discount in tuition. The lone outlier was Northwestern. It offered a *full ride*.

The end result, which came swiftly: Our Chicago public school kids are now provided the opportunity to take advantage of a path laid out for them from pre-K through four years of college. The opportunity is there. This was a huge deal for me, especially when it came to the plight of our disadvantaged children. No longer would a family have to go to the poorhouse because they were trying to provide their children with a shot at the American Dream. Where was the federal government during any of these reforms and investments? Nowhere to be found.

———

The Chicago Star Scholarship program, though only in its nascent stages, is already a smashing success. Not only is it breaking the cycle of poverty and lack of opportunity, it is also creating its own powerful, virtuous cycle. The program is attractive to high school students, and our work in their schools is supporting it. That's resulted in better and more applicants. This has made the program more attractive to colleges and universities, who are getting better students. This in turn has made those colleges and universities more attractive to employers, who are getting better employees.

Fourteen hundred high schoolers earned Star Scholarships in 2015, the program's first year. We had almost quadruple that number in the pipeline in 2018, and the number continues to grow. Nearly a thousand have gone on to the Star Plus program. The Star Scholars have done us proud: 81 percent of them are the first in their families to attend college. And they have stayed in college and graduated at nearly double the rate of their community college peers, reinforcing our 3.0 grade-point average cutoff decision.

I couldn't be prouder of the kids who have entered the program, kids like Salmo Campos. She was an excellent student, taking many AP and dual-enrollment classes, but she had to work in a law firm to help pay her bills because she had a daughter. She would have had a very difficult time affording college. But she earned a Star Scholarship, and after two free years at Richard J. Daley College, she enrolled at Northwestern in the fall of 2018.

Juan Gomez emigrated to the U.S. from Mexico when he was four years old. He was the valedictorian of his high school class at CICS Larry Hawkins, but he had no way of paying for college. His Star Scholarship provided him with two free years at Olive-Harvey College, where he excelled. He is now on track to graduate with a bachelor's degree from Northeastern Illinois University. He says his goal is to work in human resource management, and "then I definitely want to become an entrepreneur and open my own business."

Lashaunta Moore was a National Honor Society student at Percy L. Julian High School in Washington Heights. She received a Star Scholarship and matriculated to Richard J. Daley College, where she became a member of the Phi Theta Kappa Honor Society. She earned a full scholarship to Saint Xavier University and is now pursuing a degree in media communications.

Kacper Sienkiewicz, a Star Scholar, is a first-generation college student in his family. He graduated from Wilbur Wright College in the spring of 2018 and was accepted for his final two years at Northwestern, where he will continue to study physics.

And then there's Elijah Ruiz, who graduated from Whitney M.

Young Magnet High School, attended Wilbur Wright on a Star Scholarship, and then earned a full ride to Cornell University.

Without the Star Scholarship, these kids either would have had to work for a few years to make enough money to attend college—thus lessening their chances of ever going—or perhaps would have been forced to forgo college altogether. Instead they've been part of a program that has positively changed the trajectory of their lives and our city. Before I left office, we extended the Star Scholarship to students who go to parochial schools within the city. The students enrolled in the Catholic schools' Big Shoulders Fund, a program that targets poor inner-city kids and also provides free admission to community college if they have a B average. There was grumbling when I did this, but it was the right thing to do.

———

Our comprehensive education reform—from pre-K, to more schooling, to our summer programs, to the Star and Star Plus Scholarships—was one of the most rewarding things I did as mayor. These students and their future, and thus the future of Chicago, have been my biggest priority. This is why we battle. This is what makes it all worth it. We fight to give every student— regardless of income, race, gender, religion—a real chance.

This idea has caught on, as more cities and states have stepped up in the absence of ideas, leadership, and money from the federal government. Kentucky, Oregon, and Rhode Island are three states that have followed the lead of Tennessee. (Why so many states, you ask? Control of community colleges in most places is under the state government.) The Tennessee governor, Haslam, and I cowrote an op-ed in the *Wall Street Journal* in 2016 touting the efficacy of our programs. Mayor Marty Walsh in Boston has begun to offer free community college in his city, as has Louis-ville's Greg Fischer.

Think about this, though, for a moment: Not one of us working on the issues of education in community colleges and beyond got on a plane to brief the secretary of education about our plans, nor were we asked to. There were no congressional hearings on the subject. The federal government was completely absent. So, in that vacuum, we came up with the solutions, and the ideas spread among us. Individually and collectively, mayors have picked up the slack where the federal government has come up short. From free community college to universal pre-K to some of the most significant educational changes in America in the last thirty years—the federal government: MIA.

Of course, in an ideal world it would be preferable for the federal government, with its vast resources and funding, to be heavily involved in these efforts. But as with the revitalization of O'Hare International Airport and dozens of other initiatives, it was crystal clear that the cavalry would not be coming from Washington, D.C., anytime soon. For the sake of our children and their future—and ours—we decided we could no longer wait. So we did it ourselves and started to build a bridge across that yawning divide between the haves and have-nots, between that peril and that promise.

The Nation City

E ducation isn't the only space where the vacuum left by the federal government has been filled by local efforts. It isn't the only space where mayors have demonstrated that they run the most immediate, intimate, and impactful governments in the world. By ever increasing amounts, they are stepping into the vacuum left by Washington, London, and Brussels.

———

O'Hare International Airport is one of the most important transportation hubs on earth. It is the fourth-busiest airport in the world—and the busiest in the United States—handling 2,700 flights a day and some 80-plus million passengers per year and growing. As the second biggest connector airport in the world, it links to all points on the compass in the U.S. and to more than sixty foreign cities. It is the primary gateway to our city, for immigrants, business travelers, tourists, and our residents. It is one of the most significant driving forces behind Chicago's role as a vibrant city of commerce, ideas and innovation, inclusion and opportunity, a linchpin of its status as a world-class city. O'Hare, as I like to say, is Chicago's window into the world and the world's window into Chicago and beyond.

It is also, in certain critical portions, old and outdated. And this juxtaposition presents a very serious problem and opportunity.

During my two terms as mayor of Chicago, I kept two different to-do lists in a pocket in my jacket. One was a daily list, filled with the NOW attention-needing items. The second was a weekly list of items that I felt I had to deal with within those seven days. I also had a third list, one that I kept in the top drawer of the desk in my office. This one was made up of my biggest, most ambitious long-term goals during my time as mayor. I knew the decisions we made in the next two to three years would determine what Chicago looked like in the next twenty to thirty years.

The dramatic modernization of O'Hare was one of the few items that was found on all three lists. (I like lists: On the wood-paneled wall of my office, I had a framed present that President Obama had given me when I left his administration to run for mayor: his "big ideas" list for 2010.)

In 2011, the last time the lease agreement had been renegotiated, the federal government provided the city with nearly a billion dollars for the airport. But just a little more than five years later, at a critical juncture when we needed it the most? Crickets.

So I had two options when it came to modernizing O'Hare. I could cross my fingers and wait for funding from the federal government. Or I could try to figure out how we would get it done on our own.

I ended up choosing the latter. Not because I wanted to. But because I had to.

For decades the standard protocol for getting any major infrastructure plan accomplished in a city was to reach out to the federal government for both funding and guidance. That protocol no longer exists.

The federal government still talks a good game, though. On the campaign trail during the 2016 presidential election and at various times afterward, Donald Trump spoke often about his infrastructure plan for the country, touting his supposed ability as a builder. He floated big numbers—trillions of dollars in federal funding—that would be used to improve and upgrade and retrofit our nation's roads, bridges, rail lines, shipping ports, and airports.

An actual plan for achieving those numbers has never really come close to coalescing into anything concrete. What was floated was an idea to magically turn a couple hundred billion dollars into those promised trillions by leveraging local and state tax dollars and private investment. For all intents and purposes, the "plan" was just hot air, fairy dust. There was no real plan. And there may never be one.

In Chicago, we couldn't wait. We didn't have the luxury of postponing and crossing our fingers and hoping for federal help that was unlikely to ever materialize. We had to figure out our airport—out of self-interest.

So we did. In March of 2018 we announced an $8.5 billion deal for terminal and gate modernization, on top of a $1.5 billion deal for runway expansions. While we extended the airport's reach and modernized the terminals, we strengthened the bargaining rights and wages of airport workers. A very potent example of shared prosperity. The deal will dramatically expand and mod-

ernize O'Hare in what is one of the largest airport infrastructure projects in the country. We will nearly double the airport's
terminal space, adding 3 million square feet. We will build a
brand-new, state-of-the-art global alliance terminal—the first
of its kind in the U.S.—which means that international passengers with domestic connections will never have to leave the terminal. There will be new concourses and a 30 percent increase
in gates, with the capacity to expand easily when needed in the
coming decades. We will construct new runways and reconfig-
ure old ones—the equivalent of adding Midway Airport's capacity to O'Hare. And we will increase our daily international and
domestic flights by 40 percent.

Infrastructure may not be sexy, but this is a big, big deal.
Don't just take my word for it. Our hometown paper, the *Chicago Tribune*, hailed the project as a "landmark breakthrough"
and said it will "usher in a new era for Chicago." It is a project
that had to be undertaken to ensure the vibrant future of our
city. Frankly, it had to be done for the country, too. O'Hare is a
central hub in the U.S. When it doesn't function properly and
gets clogged up, the rest of the country does, too.

And here's the stunning part: We are getting this done without any new or additional economic assistance from the federal
government. We alone negotiated the deal with American Airlines and United Airlines. It wasn't always easy—the airlines felt
that they owned the airport, and effectively they were right. So
we changed a city ordinance that gave us, not them, the right
to set the rates for the costs of the gates if they did not come to
terms with the city. We gave them an offer they could not refuse:
Deal with fifty of Chicago's finest aldermen, or just the city's
aviation department. As you can imagine, they came to terms
with us pretty quickly. The deal, in the end, will be funded in

its entirety through the increase in resources generated by an increase in passenger traffic. Not a penny of new federal money, from the Department of Transportation or the Federal Aviation Administration, will be used. They of course must approve the overall plan and any environmental mitigation. We didn't ask the Department of Commerce for permission to do the deal. We didn't ask the White House or Congress, either. We negotiated directly with the airlines. In all, it took us just two years, from start to finish.

Agreements like this are becoming the norm, not the exception, and will only increase in years to come. Right now our country's largest airports—in New York and Los Angeles and here in Chicago, to name just a few—are undergoing roughly $100 billion in capital improvement projects, one of the most impressive aviation modernizations in our history. Most of them are being funded locally and with passenger traffic growth. No one is waiting around for the federal government to act anymore. And when you wait on the federal government, like the Lincoln and Holland tunnels, you just wait, and wait, and wait.

And it is unlikely that there will be much, if any, federal money for these types of projects anytime soon. The Urban Institute's C. Eugene Steuerle, in his book *Dead Men Ruling*, estimates that the U.S. federal government will be spending $4.1 trillion on our nation's entitlement programs by 2026. That won't leave much left over for anything else.

I bring up the O'Hare project not to toot my own horn (I do that plenty in the coming pages) but because I think it's a perfect illustration of what is going on around the globe right now, a huge and very consequential shift in the way the world works. National governments across the developed world have become weak, ineffective, paralyzed, dysfunctional, and those are just a few adjectives to describe what's going on. That's created a vacuum. But while national governments are receding in their role, cities and their mayors are putting points up on the board. Cities and their mayors have increasingly been required to fill that vacuum. They are the ones who are actually getting things done.

———

Chicago has always been one of Trump's favorite targets. Since 2016 he's called our city "a disaster" and said it's "out of control." He's asked, "What the hell is going on in Chicago?"

We aren't his only target, though. Trump has firmly been an anticity president, which is, of course, utterly ridiculous, since he's spent all but a few years of his life living and working in one of the great cities in the world. What Trump seems to dislike about cities is that they represent everything he's not. They are progressive, smart, dynamic, inclusive, climate-aware, healthy, innovative, and diverse, among other things. Trump has taken his dislike of cities to another level, too, holding what seems like a personal antipathy for the mayors of some of the largest cities in the world. A few of his favorite targets: Sadiq Khan in London, Anne Hidalgo in Paris, Jim Kenney in Philadelphia, and me. And the list goes on.

As it turns out, we haven't been too keen on him, either. Chicago, like other cities in the U.S., is a gateway to the American Dream, and it is open to anyone who desires to pursue that dream. We are not open, however, to those who stand in the way of that pursuit. (We punch back. Cowardly bullies don't like that very much.) In September of 2017, I rang the opening bell at Solario High School, a predominantly Hispanic school on the Southwest Side of the city, where an estimated 25 percent of the students are Dreamers ("estimated" because the city is not allowed to keep official data on the number of Dreamers in our schools). The school, which focuses on technology through a partnership with Salesforce, has a graduation rate of 92 percent. A student named Lorenzo Rivera introduced me. He is going to Northwestern. One of his brothers is also going to Northwestern. Their single mother works as a custodian. After my introduction, I declared, loud and clear, that our city was a "Trump-free zone." Yes, it was a bit of bombast. But it was also a way in which I used the bully pulpit of my office to send a strong and clear message to our citizens—and especially to those incredible students at Solario—and to the rest of the world about what we stand for and what we do not.

You can probably guess how I feel about Trump personally. But that is really beside the point. Trump is simply dead wrong about cities and mayors, in the U.S. and all over the world. He is on the wrong side of history. Our city governments, unlike his, actually work. His chaotic and incompetent White House has only served to throw this fact into greater relief. "Why did Trump ever complain about cities?" asks former New Orleans mayor Mitch Landrieu. "All he needed to do is compare records."

———

For decades now, without always really even being totally cognizant of the fact, I've been a firsthand witness to a major paradigm shift in governance.

I started my political career working for the federal level of government, from campaigning for U.S. senators to serving as a U.S. congressman to working in two different White Houses. I've been in close proximity to the most powerful person in the world's most powerful national government. I will always be proud of the work I did during my career at the federal level. I learned a lot about politics and policy and how they interact. But somewhere near the end of my fifteen-year stint at the national level, it began to dawn on me that the real lesson I was learning was about the numerous ways in which national governments no longer work.

It was while I was running the city of Chicago that I had my true epiphany and the central thesis of this book became crystal clear: Mayors effectively run the world now.

Sure, this is a bit hyperbolic, but there is more truth to it than not. Some issues, like denuclearization, military concerns, major public health risks, and our big national entitlement programs, are obviously not under the purview of mayors. But most of the day-to-day functions of the world now are. On the political front, cities are more stable. On the economic front, cities are more dynamic. On progress, cities are more effective. And on confronting challenges head on, cities act more responsibly.

Mayors run the places that are now the hubs of innovations and ideas, the places that drive the economic, intellectual, and cultural energy of the world. They acknowledge and actively address climate change. They deal with immigration and infrastructure and don't just constantly kick these issues down the road, hoping someone else will figure them out. They grapple with the challenges of education, disparities in wealth, health, housing, terrorism, and crime. Cities are globally integrated and diverse. Cities are embracing reality and creating solutions that reflect where matters are headed. Cities are all the things national governments are not. They are the present. They are also the future.

Our nation-states do not reflect our future. They are in a state of atrophy and decline. As of this writing, five national governments in Europe are run by a minority party, with perhaps a few more on the way. In a practical sense, this means that these national governments will face stagnation and gridlock as challenges mount. Things aren't much better in the U.S., which when it's not run by the minority party is still stunted by it and is polarized to the point of paralysis. In the last two decades, the only times major, impactful bills have been signed into law have been when one political party has had control of both the executive and the legislative branch. The seats of power in our nation-states have become ineffective bureaucracies, proficient only, it seems, in compounding problems by not dealing with them in a timely manner. Our national governments are fundamentally—and frustratingly—unable to address the needs and concerns of their constituents in real time.

This has had real consequences. The Trump presidency, with its constant turmoil, shadiness, and sheer ineptitude, has been a big part of the problem in the U.S. But President Trump is merely a manifestation of something much bigger, a symptom of some deeper, destructive disease. A lot of political analysts believe that the elections in and around 2016 across the globe were about economics. I disagree that the upheaval was only about economics. There was another reason people took a bat and beat the political system, whether it was Great Britain's exit from the European Union (Brexit) or the election of President Trump or the minority governments that have popped up across Europe: It was a reaction to the established nation-states' utter inability to address the fundamental issues their constituents face. The establishment had failed, and the public was willing to try anything new, no matter how nontraditional.

This is where mayors have stepped in. Our cities have become places where function has replaced dysfunction. Intimate has replaced distant, and immediate has replaced dithering. Many

Trump voters were sick of politics as usual. Mayors offer them a different way. A city's constituents can, and do, truly affect policies and outcomes through their engagement. In a Gallup poll, 35 percent of Americans surveyed said they trust the federal government. That same poll said that 72 percent trusted their local government. "Local government is where trust lives," says Eric Beinhocker, the executive director of the Institute for New Economic Thinking. It is government that touches the way residents live their lives.

We tend to train so much of our focus and energy these days on what's going on in, and what comes out of, Washington, D.C.: a president's Twitter feed, the palace intrigue, the ineffectiveness of so many congressmen and -women. To be sure, this is a totally natural human impulse. I am not dismissing some of the attention paid to the federal government: Oversight of the federal branches of government is always a must, especially when they turn out to be corrupt. I would argue, though, that we need to shift much of our focus away from Washington and direct it to places that really matter, places that are capable of moving forward to where challenges are being addressed, not ignored. We always need to keep thinking globally, of course, but we also need to understand and appreciate that most of the major issues of the world—the ones that affect us day in and day out—are actually handled locally. As Bruce Katz, cofounder of the New Localism Advisors and the founding director of the Metropolitan Policy Program at the Brookings Institution, points out, as we become more global—economically and culturally—it is not our national governments that are rising up to the task of leading the way in shaping and forming that globalism. It is our cities.

———

In 1932 the Supreme Court Justice Louis Brandeis wrote: "It is one of the happy incidents of the federal system that a single courageous state may, if its citizens choose, serve as a laboratory; and try novel social and economic experiments without risk to the rest of the country."

Justice Brandeis was, of course, exactly correct about what was going on back then. A good portion of the New Deal was cooked up in the labs of some states. Later on, the Great Society and the Affordable Care Act would be, too. These great ideas all flowed up into the national government.

Things have changed, however. Cities, not states, are now the laboratories. But, alas, those ideas no longer flow vertically (though hopefully one day the best of them will). The ideas and innovations instead are spreading horizontally from city to city, not just in the U.S. but all over the world. Idea-sharing and collaborations among cities and mayors are gaining serious momentum. In Chicago, I was a member of the Metropolitan Mayors Caucus. I was also a member of the U.S. Conference of Mayors and the global C40. Mayors work together locally, nationally, and internationally.

When Trump initiated his travel ban, hundreds of cities around the country decided to declare themselves sanctuaries for immigrants. A similar thing happened when he decided to pull the United States out of the Paris Climate Agreement. In response to his act, we held a climate conference in Chicago where dozens of the world's greatest cities decided to opt *in* to the agreement, apart from their respective national governments. Cities have become the beachhead of resistance to ill-conceived decisions of national governments that go against the popular will, protecting their citizens.

But cities and mayors don't just use that autonomy to collaborate on playing defense. The ideas generated and tested and shared are dynamic and forward-thinking *and* progressive. A new paradigm is being created, and cities—with collaborations among their citizens, universities, nonprofits, and foundations— and their mayors are at the heart of it. This new paradigm is replacing the old federal-local partnership.

When former New York City mayor Michael Bloomberg created a technology hub with partnerships among universities, businesses, and the local government, scores of other cities— including Chicago—decided to do the same thing. Our idea to sue big pharmaceutical companies for deceptive marketing when no one else was really addressing the opioid epidemic caught on quickly. More than seven hundred other cities are now involved in lawsuits. The Riverwalk project we built on the Chicago River was informed by what we saw happening concurrently on the waterfronts of Paris and Berlin and Dallas and Buenos Aires. This idea of repurposing old industrial waterfronts in cities has since spread across the world. Tackling public education as a holistic, prekindergarten-through-college initiative rose nearly simultaneously here in Chicago and in Louisville and Boston. "Good mayors imitate," says Dayton, Ohio, mayor Nan Whaley. "Great mayors steal."

These collaborations have proliferated and accelerated "just as the ability of our national politicians to work together has ground to a halt," says Bruce Katz. Cities, for all intents and purposes, are on their own now. As major deliverers of goods, they don't have the luxury or patience to wait to solve problems. Cities are collectively plotting independent courses and learning from each other to solve problems. This is happening, as you'll see, in cities that are large (Chicago), medium (Louisville), and small (Carmel, Indiana). They work together, outside of their respective national governments. They trade goods, ideas, and innovations. They've become nation cities.

And here's another thing that's going on in cities and with mayors that's in direct contrast to what's happening on the national level: Cities and mayors are governing effectively, and they are sharing ideas on a nonpartisan level. Though many of the biggest cities in the world are led by mayors who identify as liberals, many are not. Through the U.S. Conference of Mayors and other intermediaries both domestic and international, we all work together, regardless of political labels. There is a reason for this: We all face the same problems, and we all must deal with them immediately. "We maybe come from different broader philosophical ideas about the role of government," says Tom Tait, the Republican former mayor of Anaheim. "But at the local level it's about getting things done and serving people. And there's not a whole lot of ideology in that." Says Knox White, the Republican mayor of Greenville, South Carolina, "Our federal politicians are in a bubble. We aren't on the city level, and don't want to be. We talk to our constituents. We work with each other to get things done. My job is to facilitate this. It's what I do. That's what a mayor does."

Being a mayor is pragmatic and political, but it's not partisan. It's about looking forward and not backward. It's about the locally progressive politics that truly make a positive difference in people's lives.

———

In late 2018, I announced that I would not seek a third term as the mayor of Chicago. It was a difficult decision. It was the best job I've ever had, an honor and a privilege. But after twenty-four years in politics, I realized it was time to take a break. Though

I still believed I could effectively run the city, I realized that I wouldn't be able to give the people of Chicago what they deserve from their mayor—which is me giving everything I have every single day for four more years. In our present moment, this is what cities demand, need, and deserve from their mayors. So I knew it was time to step away. I may come back to electoral politics one day. Or I may not. I'll take my time to try to figure that out.

What I do know is that I've seen it all, from the halls of Congress to the West Wing to the Oval Office, to the fifth floor of Chicago's City Hall. The view from that fifth-floor office was by far the best, because I'm an activist and a center-left progressive and want to have intimate and effective impacts on the lives and well-being of people, and be able to put my thumb on the scale, and tip the scale to a more inclusive city.

Being a mayor these days is the most important job in politics. Mayors and cities all over the world are stepping in where their national governments have stepped back, or even completely turned their backs and walked away. The poison in our national governments has made our politics sick. Mayors are working every day to bring it all back to health.

THREE

How Did We Get Here?

In 2013 the late Benjamin Barber wrote a book titled *If Mayors Ruled the World*. With the declining nation-state and the corresponding rise of the city, the conditional part of the title is no longer needed. It's happening right now.

Of course, the path there was rather long and tortuous.

———

"When the burdens of the presidency seem unusually heavy, I always remind myself it could be worse," Lyndon Baines Johnson said in 1966. "I could be a mayor."

At the time in our history when LBJ uttered those words, he was absolutely correct. American cities were combusting, some quite literally.

Rumblings of what would become a riotous era in the fight for civil rights that was as bloody as it was momentous started in the summer of 1964. In mid-July of that summer, in the Harlem section of New York City, the shooting of an unarmed fifteen-year-old African American young man by a police officer triggered six days of rioting. A few days later, after an incident of alleged police brutality, riots broke out in Rochester, New York, and they were quelled only after then-governor Nelson Rockefeller called in the National Guard. One month later the rumored beating death of a pregnant African American woman set off two days of rioting in Philadelphia, during which incensed mobs of African American men burned and looted mostly white-owned businesses in the city.

The tumult only intensified over the ensuing years. The six-day riot in the Watts section of Los Angeles in 1965 was the largest of the civil rights era, resulting in thirty-four deaths and more than $40 million in damages ($325 million in today's dollars). During what became known as the "long, hot summer" of 1967, more than 150 American cities experienced riots. The deadliest took place in Detroit, leaving 43 dead, 342 seriously injured, and more than 1,400 buildings looted or burned.

After Martin Luther King, Jr., was assassinated in April 1968, riots occurred in more than a hundred U.S. cities. One of those cities was Chicago. I remember that riot. (You may notice some of the parallels between these riots and the unrest in recent years here in America, in Ferguson and Baltimore and Milwaukee and Charlotte. Racial tensions still exist. Though we've made some progress, our system is not perfect, and mayors work on it every day. I get into Chicago's efforts in a later chapter.)

But race riots were only one of the problems vexing our cities in the 1960s and '70s. In 1969 parts of Cleveland's heavily polluted Cuyahoga River caught fire. Boston was thrown into chaos over its school busing policies in 1974. New York City verged on a disaster of its own making as it spiraled toward bankruptcy in 1975 and then-president Gerald Ford responded by pledging to veto any federal bailout of the city. (This prompted the famous

New York Daily News headline "Ford to City: Drop Dead.") Two years later the Bronx burned during a blackout and the riots that followed.

European cities were also in trouble at the time. London was besieged in the 1970s by Provisional Irish Republican Army (IRA) terrorism, blackouts, and strikes. Paris suffered through serious crime waves and high unemployment. Copenhagen was nearly bankrupt and 18 percent of its population was unemployed. Even cities in the Far East were suffering: Singapore went through a series of race riots and bombings in the mid-1960s during its transition to becoming a republic.

Our cities were in crisis thanks mostly to the intertwined, three-headed monster of racial segregation, depopulation, and deindustrialization. The latter was the tip of the spear. As the era of the industrial city came to a close—with manufacturing jobs and businesses moving to the suburbs, the South, or overseas— many city-dwellers lost their jobs or experienced steep declines in wages. Detroit alone lost 40 percent of its industrial jobs in the 1970s. That job loss, coupled with a mid-1970s recession and high interest rates, left cities . . . well, for the dead.

Many of the millions of African Americans who had mi- grated north in search of jobs and an escape from the oppressive South soon found little, if any, succor in their new homes. Afri- can Americans were often grouped in neighborhoods undesired by the better-off whites, and the prospects of improving those neighborhoods—and thus their lives—were dampened by rac- ist practices such as redlining, which denied or limited loans to people in certain neighborhoods, most of whom happened to be African Americans. It didn't help, of course, that the riots left some already blighted neighborhoods in far worse shape.

The riots, the rising crime rate, and the loss of jobs "helped create a sense that civilization had fled the cities," Edward Glaeser wrote in his 2011 book, *Triumph of the City*. So, many city-dwellers themselves fled, in what became known as "white flight," and businesses—even those outside the manufacturing industry—began to follow them. The great escape was made easier by the concurrent growth of planned suburbs and the completion of a federal highway system. Cleveland's population fell 37 percent from 1950 to 1980. Boston's dropped 30 percent, and Chicago's 17 percent. This significant depopulation made the situation in cities even worse, leading to falling tax revenues— there were fewer people to tax, and those who had stayed behind were, generally speaking, poorer than those who had left. Infrastructure and mass transit systems and other critical city services (like public education and policing) were some of the casualties. Our major cities had lower life expectancy rates than the country as a whole.

It didn't help that city planners from decades earlier had been misguided in some of their approaches. Jane Jacobs, in her 1961 book, *The Death and Life of Great American Cities,* wrote about one of the biggest problems cities faced: Most urban planning had been focused on business districts and not on building and strengthening the neighborhoods and communities that form the glue that holds cities together. It also didn't help that some of the mayors of that period were not up to the task. New York City mayor John Lindsay, who served from 1966 to 1973, never could rein in the city's costs. He also was unable to work out deals with the city's transit and sanitation workers and teachers and endured four devastating strikes in his first term. Jerome Cavanagh, the mayor of Detroit from 1962 to 1970, tried to build his way out of his city's fiscal mess when what his city needed was investments in the growth of new industries and people with innovative ideas. Neither of these two mayors was effective at fighting crime in his city.

All of this—the racial segregation, the deindustrialization, the depopulation, the higher taxes, the crumbling services, the general loss of faith—led, of course, to *more* social upheaval. Cities were caught in a downward spiral, an unvirtuous cycle that seemed to have no end. Urban America was, literally and spiritually, burning and hollowing out.

It seems almost unfathomable now to believe that these cities have risen from the ashes to become the economic and cultural hubs of the world, to become beehives of activity, creativity, and progressivism. But they have. Now, in fact, it is the great nation-states that are falling apart. Fifty years ago mayors went to Washington, D.C., on bended knee, begging to be saved and bailed out. Today, fifty years later, mayors are trying to save all of us *from* Washington, D.C., and D.C. from itself.

———

Upon the founding of the United States of America, the emphasis was on the "states" part of the country's name. The country was formed by the original thirteen colonies. Our first national governing agreement, ratified in 1781, was the Articles of Confederation, which basically allowed the states to do their own thing in every aspect of governing save for dealing with foreign affairs and territorial issues. Six years later our founders met again and decided that a state-led national government wasn't the best choice. They drew up what we now call the Constitution and ratified it in 1788. That document, and the Bill of Rights, are responsible for the setup of our federally led system.

Yet states still held much sway for nearly another century. The federal government was small and rather weak. Westward expansion was accomplished by forming new states, and because of a void in federal law (and a lack of power), the central question for each of the new states was whether it would be free or slaveholding.

The battle over that question eventually led to the Civil War (also known as the War Between the States by some on the losing side), which began when a group of states banded together and seceded from the federal union. Those southern states desired stronger rights (so they could continue to own slaves) at the expense of a weaker federal government. They got them, at least for a while. The preamble of the Confederate Constitution begins with the phrase "We, the people of the Confederate States, each State acting in its sovereign and independent character . . ." The document also contains several provisions that grant some of the federal power found in the U.S. Constitution back to the states.

The outcome of the Civil War put an end to the dominance of states in the U.S. government system. Through some fits and starts, federal influence began to grow from that point on. The first two projects beyond Reconstruction after the Civil War, transcontinental railroad development and the land grant college system, illustrate the point.

———

The great nation-state of the United States of America begins with the country's response to the Great Depression. Franklin Delano Roosevelt's New Deal remains one of our nation's greatest achievements, a shining example of how the federal government can work on behalf of its citizens and benefit them in a progressive manner. World War II—its ramp-up and eventual victory—galvanized the nation into collective action and demonstrated what good could be accomplished. Federal programs such as Social Security, wage laws and union protection, and the GI Bill rose after the Depression and World War II. Federal money began to flow, with great effect, into research and university education, resulting in programs like NASA. The military-industrial complex that Dwight D. Eisenhower warned us about came to fruition and became, for better or worse, a demonstration of rich and purposeful federal government. Through the nation's growth and our great social technologies—like the rule of law—the federal system originally constructed by our Founding Fathers became "in some ways the first continent-wide economy," says Eric Beinhocker of the Institute for New Economic Thinking. Then came the civil rights era and the Great Society, as our nation-state reached for its apex.

The default mode of the federal government then was consensus-building. After World War II, "progress" didn't come from one political party's philosophy but from the two major parties working together on compromise around essential consensus on America's purpose. Our nation-state was built on an implicit agreement: that it would strive to work for the benefit of all of its citizens. It was never perfect, of course. But to paraphrase Martin Luther King, Jr., the arc of the nation-state's moral universe, though long, always bent toward justice and progress.

———

Think for a moment about the incredible progress delivered by the federal government after World War II, the vast majority of it in a bipartisan manner. The Marshall Plan came together in 1948 under a Democratic president (Harry S. Truman) and a Republican Congress. In 1956, President Eisenhower worked with a Democratic Congress to create what was a *real* infrastructure program—the Federal Aid Highway Act, better known as the Interstate Highway System. When Lyndon Baines Johnson proposed the Great Society and civil rights legislation, many conservatives were displeased, believing it to be an overreach of the federal government. But a compromise was achieved, and subsequent *Republican* presidents—Richard Nixon and Gerald Ford—ended up expanding the programs during their terms. (This prompted Nixon's famous "I am now a Keynesian in economics" line.) There was the formation of Medicare and Medicaid, and the Clean Air and Clean Water Acts, and the War on Poverty. All of them were worked on as compromises. In 1986, Ronald Reagan's Tax Reform Act was sponsored by Dan Rostenkowski, who was a Democratic representative.

The art of compromise—really, the art of the executive branch of government working with the legislative one to conquer evil, fix problems, and respond to constituents—continued all the way into Bill Clinton's second term. I was present when the Children's Health Insurance Program and the balanced budget were passed with support from the Republican-controlled Congress in 1997. We also passed a comprehensive welfare reform bill and the assault-weapons ban and accomplished an expansion of the North Atlantic Treaty Organization (NATO) to eastern Europe.

It wasn't that long ago when the nation-state was a source of strength, an immensely positive, consensus-building force. It didn't always work perfectly, but it did *work* . . . until it didn't.

———

The retreat of our nation-state was more *evolutionary* than *revolutionary* in nature. There was no single point of inflection, but rather an assortment of events and circumstances that, taken together over a period of time, have led to dysfunction in the

cooperative structure of the federal government. That dysfunction has compounded with an unraveling of trust between the
public and the government.

Beginning with Barry Goldwater and Richard Nixon, the modern Republican Party has invested time and resources in feed-
ing public resentment of intellectual and cultural elites, which
began to sow seeds of distrust of those in power. (The irony here,
that Nixon and his crew were part of that elite *and actually warranted distrust,* is not lost.) The party also began to feed fear of
the "other" (read: immigrants and racial and religious minorities) in our modern America. This resentment would only blos-
som in the ensuing years, culminating in the election of a certain
president.

Vietnam, with the uncertainty of its mission, the secrecy
with which it was handled (for example, the bombing in Cam-
bodia), and the tens of thousands of lives that were ruined for
no gain, added to the level of distrust. Subsequent decades-long
wars in Iraq (which we entered into on the basis of evidence that
turned out to be false) and Afghanistan have furthered suspi-
cions about the federal government's wisdom when it comes to
foreign wars. Watergate was, of course, a seminal moment in the
fall of our nation-state. (There is a reason that the suffix "-gate" is
now added to nearly every misdeed in the government and elsewhere.) The scandal was a defining wound on our federal government, changing the way citizens of the United States viewed
their federal government and the people who were in charge of
it. There's still a deep scar.

Reagan somehow turned this around to his benefit, running
and governing on distrust by portraying the very government
that he led as evil and problematic (again, the irony) while con-

tinuing to rail against the "elites" and continuing to side with big business. As James Fallows of *The Atlantic* has pointed out, this has left our electorate in a strange place, where poor white voters in, say, Kansas or West Virginia "support tax policies that disproportionally support financiers in New York and San Francisco."

From that point on, the issues with the federal government began to snowball. Reagan's Federal Communications Commission chairman revoked what's known as the fairness doctrine in broadcasting, a policy that had been put in place in 1949 that guaranteed the airing of different views on issues of significant public interest. Revoking this doctrine led to the rise of Fox News and the Sinclair Broadcast Group (the largest owner of television stations in the U.S.), both of which have capitalized on the moneymaking opportunities presented by airing harshly partisan news on the Republican side. When the left later countered with MSNBC, the balkanization of the news—and the information spreading and inflaming partisanship that came with it—was complete. This led to an opening for a presidential candidate like, say, Donald Trump to publicly describe any news that he didn't like as "fake." In recent years the explosion of social media, with its filter bubbles, its fast-spreading conspiracy theories, its vulnerability to hacking, its easily doctored photos, and its proliferation of ill-thought-out hot takes, has only exacerbated this problem, to the point where it just might have swung a presidential election.

Aggressive gerrymandering, which began to increase in the early 2000s, has also played a big role in the nation-state's decline. It has increased partisanship. It has destroyed natural competition, which has eroded the performance and accountability of elected officials and the confidence of the electorate, which feels as if the entire system is rigged (and basically, when it comes to gerrymandering, it is).

And speaking of partisanship, some of today's problems we have in the federal government are the fault of one man: Newt Gingrich, who was the Republican Speaker of the House from 1995 until 1999, when, thankfully, he resigned. Gingrich did something that no one before him had ever done: He weaponized his position and politics and undermined democratic norms along the way. He practiced brinkmanship, not unlike that seen between the United States and the Soviet Union during the Cold War. That tit-for-tat style of governing led to the collapse of bipartisanship.

Money, of course, is at the heart of the problem. It has flown out the door in the form of national debt. Entitlement programs have become more costly. Wars happen to be expensive, too (and wars entered into on false premises are even more expensive). But it is the money flowing into politics—which has the political class firmly in its grasp—that's the more significant problem. Thanks to the Supreme Court's irresponsible and nearly inconceivable *Citizens United* decision in 2010, the influence of big money, sometimes from unknown and undisclosed "dark" sources, has grown immensely. There is a feeling now among the electorate that billionaires, like the Koch brothers and Sheldon Adelson on the right and George Soros on the left, now pull the strings of the federal government. Perhaps those fears are warranted. In 2014 two professors, Martin Gilens from Princeton and Benjamin I. Page from Northwestern, published a paper that basically contended that our federal government had already become an oligarchy. I know of a certain president who wouldn't mind that.

Biased news, gerrymandering, and money have made fierce and intractable partisanship the norm and have left us with a federal government that is oxygenated by confrontation and not compromise. This led to the inevitable: a federal government that was no longer working for its citizens. Yes, there have been bills passed and programs enacted since the Clinton years that make it seem like the federal government is actually working. But the vast majority of them have come when a single party has controlled the federal government. That can-do spirit of compromise and working together for all the citizens of the country, not just a portion of them, ended during the presidency of George W. Bush.

I was a congressman then, and we did have moments very early on when we all did work together (the 9/11 attacks united us for a while). But those moments were fleeting. Bush really had a productive presidency, getting his tax cuts and his wars, only when the Republicans also controlled Congress. And that came to a sudden halt in 2006, when the Democrats captured the House.

By the time Obama took office, the federal government was broken. We tried to fix it, but we couldn't. Just before we got into office, Obama signed on to the Troubled Asset Relief Program (TARP) initiated by Bush. We also got major stimulus, health-care, and financial reform bills passed in Obama's first two years, when our party also controlled Congress (and we had an incredible chief of staff, who will remain nameless). But we still paid a terrible political price for some of those bills, because of the electorate's widespread distrust of the federal government. They were appropriate policies, but the politics backfired.

Let me explain: The TARP bill bailed out the financial system. Obama's decision to sign on for that was made carefully and with much forethought (as all of his decisions were). The feeling was that the system was so stressed that it verged on total collapse. Obama feared that going after the banks could possibly cause an economic Armageddon. So he opted for the safer and smarter route. We also bailed out the auto industry. This bailout was designed to help the middle class as much as anyone.

But to the middle class, which bore the brunt of the 2008 mortgage collapse, it looked like some of the major perpetrators in a nationwide fraud were getting off scot-free. I still believe it was the right thing to do. But the political optics were terrible, and we paid a price for it. According to a Pew Research Center study, almost half of Americans believed the TARP bill was Obama's and not Bush's—of course. The auto industry bailout was perceived in the same manner. The middle class believed it was a get-out-of-jail-free card intended solely for the executives who created the crisis in the first place.

And then came the Affordable Care Act. Again, this was a great piece of social policy. We had to provide health-care coverage for the 40 million formerly uninsured people in our country. The program at one level was an expansion of Medicaid for the working poor, but our political opposition painted it as health care for "others" while you struggled to pay your own bills. People also came to believe that they would *lose* their health care and doctor and not be able to keep them as promised. Somehow those narratives became the more accepted ones—at the time.

These two bills, coupled with a deep recession, left the country with a middle class that felt squeezed. People in the middle class already believed, according to polls, that for the first time in America's history, their children's future would be worse than theirs. The way they perceived it, they were working hard every day to send their kids to college and make ends meet, and no one in the class above them went to jail for helping to cause the Great Recession, and the government was messing with their health care. Basically they said, "Screw it all."

So what we ended up with was an electorate that had even less trust in the federal government and a full-fledged middle-class, populist revolt. That helped end the flurry of activity in the Obama White House, which came to an end in 2010 when Tea Party–led Republicans again took control of Congress. The good policy and bad politics had other unintended consequences, too. It's part of the reason we ended up with a disastrous anomaly like President Trump.

What I believe was the bitter end of good-faith compromise in Washington, D.C., came next. It happened when Obama nominated Merrick Garland for the Supreme Court seat that had opened when Antonin Scalia died. Obama purposely did not nominate a liberal judge. Garland was a centrist. But the Republican-led Senate refused even to hold hearings about his nomination, a bold rejection of its constitutional duty. Consensus-building had already appeared to be dead for a while, but this action (or inaction, as it were) shoveled the last bits of dirt on its grave.

Both Bush and Obama resorted to executive orders when they could no longer get things done with Congress, which is not exactly the ideal manner of governance. It also makes it fairly easy for a succeeding president to undo many of his predecessor's actions and thus helps lead to what we have going on now with each presidential election cycle: a never-ending ping-pong match, where Bush reverses many of Clinton's initiatives, then Obama dismantles many of Bush's, and so on. This is neither an effective nor a healthy way for our federal government to operate.

These trends have continued with the Trump administration, and his unpopularity and incompetence have only made everything worse. His only "successes"—getting Neil Gorsuch and Brett Kavanaugh on the Supreme Court and getting a tax reform bill passed—happened because his party also controlled Congress. Just imagine for a moment Trump trying to pass the tax reform bill or trying to get Kavanaugh onto the Supreme Court with a Democratic Senate. Or, for that matter, imagine Obama trying to get the stimulus and health-care bills through a Republican Congress. (The fact that you probably can't even picture any of these things ever happening is the problem.) Trump, too, has resorted to executive orders. He did so much earlier than either Bush or Obama did, even when his party controlled both houses of Congress, a sign of his weakness and the wrongheadedness of his policies. Of course, he has been much less successful with his executive orders than his predecessors were, with many of his being held up in the courts.

I have to stop here and mention a thought that was relayed to me by my friend Amy Liu at the Brookings Institution. She points out that the federal government—and especially Trump's administration—is actually occasionally functional for *some* people in the country. Trump's presidency has been a boon for polluters and white supremacists, for example. She's undeniably correct. But, thankfully, these people are in the tiniest of minorities in this country, wildly unpopular. And if the federal government appeals to and works for them, it is by definition broken.

So where has all of this left our federal government? In essence, it has become merely a defense budget, a retirement plan, and an intentionally hobbled health-care plan. That's about it. There are no longer any substantial ideas. There are no substantial investments—or, really, any attempts to invest—in the future. Investments in research and development at the federal level have shrunk consistently over the years, apart from President Obama's stimulus bill. Our federal government is sclerotic, clumsy, inflexible, wounded, and weak, unable to move forward. This is not just happening here in the United States. The other big vote in 2016—Brexit—was essentially Great Britain's decision to no longer try to build consensus with its European neighbors. To be sure, the European Union capital, Brussels, feels just as remote and faceless and bureaucratic to its citizens as Washington, D.C., does to Americans. There really is no feeling of connection, and that's part of the problem.

I do want to make one thing clear here: I am not anti–national government. I would like nothing more than to see our national government and those around the world function well and work on behalf of their people, addressing the challenges they face and investing in the future they want to make. The heart of progressivism is a functioning government that the public believes is also an affirmative force for good. At the very least, progressives (and everyone else) should expect a national government to take the lead on education, infrastructure, research, and protections (military, environmental, and public health). These responsibilities have been slipping from our federal government's grasp in recent decades. It is my hope that someday we will have a federal government that does these things again. But it's not happening now. The ability of our nation-states to organize modern, liberal democracies is cracking. With that, people have been forced to look for alternatives.

I witnessed the fall of the nation-state from a front-row seat. I left that seat because I knew I could do more for people—in a place where government is more immediate, intimate, and impactful.

FOUR

The Rise of Cities

I n October 2017, I attended a C40 Climate Leadership conference in Mexico City. As the name suggests, the C40 is
a global partnership of cities that have united to tackle
the issue of climate change. It's one of the more significant intermediary groups of mayors who work outside their national governments, representing more than ninety of the world's biggest
cities, which govern more than 650 million people worldwide.

Needless to say, the issue that the C40 concerns itself with is a
very important one. I always made it a point to attend the organization's meetings during my time as mayor. But none of the
previous meetings had had quite the same feeling of urgency as
this one. The reason was an action taken by the U.S. government.

Two months earlier, Donald Trump had delivered a memo to
the United Nations informing that international body that the
United States—which is responsible for close to 15 percent of
the world's greenhouse gas emissions—was withdrawing from
the Paris Climate Agreement. That agreement, an international
effort to reduce worldwide greenhouse gas emissions, had been

drawn up in 2015–16 and was eventually signed by 194 countries, including the U.S. under President Obama. Though not perfect, the agreement was, by most accounts, a definitive progressive step forward in addressing our planet's most threatening problem—a fundamental call to arms.

And now our country was, suddenly and stupidly, no longer part of it.

During that C40 meeting in Mexico City, I met with Mark Watts, the executive director of the organization. "This is such an idiotic decision by our federal government," I told him. "I don't know about you, but I'm tired of going to these conferences where we all talk a lot and nothing ever comes of it." He agreed. So we decided that we needed to do something decisive to counter Trump's disastrous decision. We hit on the idea of a climate change meeting of mayors to be held in North America, one in which we would agree on a new course of action. I offered to host the meeting in Chicago.

And so, months later, fifty mayors—including, among others, Anne Hidalgo of Paris, Denis Coderre of Montreal, Miguel Ángel Mancera of Mexico City, myself, and close to forty other North American mayors—met in Chicago and signed a climate document that bound each of our cities to uphold the Paris Agreement. The Chicago Climate Charter, as it came to be known, was not just some fluffy photo opportunity (by the way, I'm not averse to those). Each of the eventual eighty cities of all sizes from all over the world signed its own customized and measurable agreement plan. We all signed on to the same destination (the 2025 goals laid out by the Paris Agreement), but we would each get there in our own individual ways, following our own road map for reducing greenhouse emissions. This seemed a more prudent and effective tactic than just signing one boilerplate document. My plan for Chicago, for instance, involved a widespread retrofitting of office buildings, plus the closing of two coal plants. Paris focused on mass transit. Vancouver aimed to reduce its use of fossil fuels and replace them with renewable energy.

It has worked, too. More than half of the cities that signed the pledge have reduced their greenhouse gas emissions, even as their populations and economies have grown. This wasn't just posturing. It was a direct rebuttal of Trump's regressive policies and tactics with a plan of action.

It was also a demonstration of the power that cities hold in this day and age. It should not be lost on anyone that mayors were acting in a multilateral way, while Trump was taking a unilateral approach. Collectively we defied the wishes of what is supposedly the most powerful man on earth. Chicago flexed its muscles again when Trump's Environmental Protection Agency took down its website about climate change. I directed Chicago to post all of the scientific data about climate change on our city site instead. Then I called other mayors and urged them to follow suit, to post research done by their universities or by the cities themselves. Many other cities did, and in that way cities filled the void left by the federal government.

Another example: When Trump issued his immigration ban and started to harass immigrants who were already in the United States, some sixty cities—from Birmingham, Alabama, to Burlington, Vermont—declared themselves "sanctuary cities" for immigrants. (I prefer to call Chicago a "welcoming city.") Trump, being the heavy-handed bully he is, tried to withhold federal funding for these cities, but the courts to date have rebuffed his attempts.

But this isn't all about Trump or a resistance. As I said before,

Trump is merely a symptom of a disease at the federal level. He has been a particularly bad symptom—I hope not a lethal one—but merely an exemplar of the trouble and dysfunction currently plaguing the nation-state.

———

The nation-state is a relative newcomer on the global stage, just three hundred to four hundred years old. Contrast that to the city, which historians agree began to take shape sometime during the Neolithic Revolution some 10,000 years ago, as our hunter-gatherer ancestors became agricultural and created more permanent settlements. Rome, for instance, has been a city for at least 2,800 years. (Don't worry—this will be quick, just proving to my parents that Sarah Lawrence gave me a good education.)

This is not to say that older is necessarily better. But cities have been through countless ups and downs in the last few thousand years. That they were able to rise again out of the ashes of the riots of the 1960s and 1970s should come as no surprise. In his book *Triumph of the City,* Edward Glaeser points out that riots in cities are more often than not tipping points, signs that change is not only needed but on its way. The Boston Massacre in 1770 and the Boston Tea Party three years later foreshadowed the coming Revolutionary War, just as the race riots in various American cities marked a turning point in the civil rights era. The issues in our cities from the 1960s through the 1980s—crime, race relations, failing schools, falling investments, and crumbling infrastructure—needed immediate attention, and the attention given to them started a revival. By then the nation-state had washed its hands of these problems. This was made loud and clear by Reagan's consolidation of block grants in the 1980s, which stanched the flow of federal money to urban areas.

Problem-solving was going to be left to the cities. And solving problems is exactly what they did, as cities began their rise just as the nation-state began to recede.

———

In the late 1980s and early 1990s, the population losses of the previous decades in our major world cities began to level off. By the early 2000s, cities began to post slight gains in population. And then, sometime in the middle of the first decade of the century, an enormous change in human migration started to take place, such that by the end of that decade an estimated 3 million people were moving to urban areas around the world *every week,* according to the United Nations. By 2050, it is believed, two out of every three people in the world will live in cities. In just three decades, cities shifted from being places people were fleeing from to places people were flocking to. They'd become places where people could live, work, and play. And the cities that find the right equilibrium among those three qualities will be the ones that prosper in the future.

Economics have been a major driver. The world's economy, once somewhat parceled and provincial, started to become truly global after World War II, fueled by the technological changes that came from the war. Technology made the exchange of goods, services, and workers much easier, and it soon became a replacement for manufacturing in cities. The hyperglobal, technology-based economy really began to thrive in the 1990s, taking cities right along with it. The world became, somewhat paradoxically, more global economically and more local politically at the same time. It's one reason cities can make the most of globalization for their residents. Like the Internet, the global economy is nothing more, really, than the sum of its many smaller parts, an accumulation of its nodes. The nodes in this case are cities, and as Bruce Katz has pointed out, the global economy now is really just an aggregation of city economies.

In the U.S. alone, metropolitan areas are responsible for 85 percent of the country's gross domestic product and jobs. And speaking of the Internet, that technology was supposed to free up workers to live and work wherever they wanted. In theory, you could now work for a New York City financial services firm by telecommuting from a farm in Vermont. While some people have pulled that off, by and large the opposite has occurred. The new digital technology economy has instead clustered its workers together and given a whole new importance and relevance to proximity and density and the sharing of ideas and services that comes with that. Those places of proximity and density are, of course, our cities. From the 1960s through the 1980s, that density worked against cities. It resulted in conflagrations of violence and protest. People wanted space, so they moved to the suburbs. Now that density is one of the great assets of our cities. People want to be close to work, to be able to walk to school and their jobs. As we have continued to build and rebuild our parks, libraries, schools, bike lanes, and mass transit systems, that density has only become more of a strength.

What's ensued is a virtuous cycle, sustained by mutual reinforcement: Companies began setting up in or moving back to cities, because that's where the potential employees were, and potential employees moved to cities because that's where the companies were. GE Healthcare Worldwide, GE Transportation, ConAgra, Oscar Mayer, Kraft Heinz, and Wilson Sporting Goods have all moved their headquarters to Chicago in recent years. McDonald's—which fled for the suburbs during the turbulent 1970s—moved its headquarters back to the city. Google,

IBM, Microsoft, and Salesforce, to name just a few, have a significant presence in Chicago now. This is happening in cities everywhere.

As an offshoot of this phenomenon, universities and research facilities have built up their presences in cities, drawing talented students and faculty from all over the world and producing potential employees, entrepreneurs, and inventions. This clustering of companies and universities and research facilities and employees has created what's known as an agglomeration economy, one that benefits all entities involved through cost savings and efficiencies. Partnerships between cities and these entities have boomed. This has all had a huge positive effect on our cities, for tax revenues and human capital and new ideas and innovations.

Cities don't just benefit the white-collar businesses and their college-educated employees. There is opportunity for all. In cities, the rich and the poor commute and work together and, in many places, live in close proximity. (Affordable housing remains a real problem, of course, and I address this in a bit.) Too many associate poverty with big cities, ignoring the fact that the poor come to big cities for the opportunity to improve their lives. There is also a near-perfect correlation, Glaeser notes, "between urbanization and prosperity across nations. On average, as the share of a country's population that is urban rises 10 percent, the country's per capita output increases 30 percent."

This new economic opportunity has dovetailed with cities becoming better places to live. There's a bit of a chicken-and-egg thing going on here. Did cities realize population increases because they became more livable? Or did they become more livable because population increases demanded it? I think it's a mix of both. Though we still have a ways to go with racial relations, things started getting a bit better in that area in the 1990s. Crime rates fell, thanks to more effective community policing and the use of more data in crime-fighting that had an emphasis on preventing crimes rather than just responding to them. I give credit to Police Chief William Bratton for a data-driven crime-fighting strategy that changed policing in America. Bratton instituted the "broken windows" method of stopping crime in New York City, in which nabbing people for small crimes led to a drastic decrease in larger ones. (Rudolph Giuliani, then the mayor, eventually took it all too far, of course, with his overaggressive stop-and-frisk policies, but Bratton's initial method remains a good one.) New York City is emblematic of most cities in this country in terms of falling crime rates. In the 1990s the city had 14.6 murders per 100,000 people. In 2016 that had dropped to 3.4 murders per 100,000 people.

I did not come to the job of mayor as a stranger to community policing and gun control. I helped pass the assault-weapons ban, the Brady Bill, and funding for 100,000 community police officers.

In Chicago, too, our crime has dropped drastically since the 1960s, '70s, and '80s. (It still remains an issue, though, and I delve into this in a later chapter.) AmericanViolence.org, a nonprofit research group led by Patrick Sharkey, a New York University professor and one of the world's foremost experts on crime, notes that there was a 57 percent decrease in the murder rate in seventy-eight of the nation's largest cities from 1991 to 2017. Despite a recent small uptick in violence in cities, the general trend has been a substantial decline in urban violence starting in the mid-1990s.

Dropping crime rates aren't the only enticement to live in a city. The physical spaces of cities have improved dramatically in the last three decades. Mayors and cities began to repurpose old industrial sites, turning them into playgrounds and parks. They focused on reducing car traffic by rebuilding mass transit systems and making cities more walkable and bikeable. Cities were the primary beneficiaries of the Clean Air Act (in the 1960s) and the Clean Water Act (in the 1970s), which have improved air quality and cleaned up waterways. (The Cuyahoga River is no longer flammable. Los Angeles's air quality has dramatically improved. When I was growing up, we used to have to run into the water, dive underneath, hold our breath, and swim thirty feet to get past all the dead fish that had washed ashore. That no longer happens.) Retail establishments, restaurants, and cultural institutions have flourished, making cities more attractive to the young, to new families, and to empty-nesters. The service economy has flourished, which favors cities, where people congregate and there is an increased demand for services.

Speaking of young people, they've been part of a general demographic trend that has pushed along the livability and dynamism of cities. Young people are waiting longer and longer to settle down and have children. Many of them, seeking employment and potential partners, have moved to cities, where they can find both. And many of those who move to cities decide to stay even after settling down to have children, because the cities have become better places to live. That act, of course, reinforces this livability. In Chicago, where in the past decades we saw white flight, we have now seen our populations of white, Hispanic, and Asians increase. (That is not true for African Americans, where we have much more work to do, as I will explain later on.)

Cities have also become attractive because of what they stand for. Minorities and the LGBTQ+ community, to name just two groups, have come to cities because of their inclusivity and progressivism. In cities there is far less fear of the "other." Multitudes of people of different races, backgrounds, and religious and sexual identities interact every day. Cities stand up for the ideas that most progressive people in the world believe in: equal rights for all, gun control, the strength of diversity, protection for immigrants, addressing climate change, good public education, economic opportunity, and inclusive economic strategies. "Cities are the world," says Amy Liu of the Brookings Institution. "The world is becoming hyperdiverse, innovative, global, and digital. And this is what cities represent." I think this is true, even as some of our national governments reflect the opposite.

Because of their density, cities are places of innovation and competition, agglomerations of economies, ideas, and cultures. Ideas and talent are shared and built upon. This is the way it's always been. Socrates, Plato, and Aristotle all rose to prominence in Athens. The Renaissance, with Leonardo da Vinci and Michelangelo, bloomed in Florence. The industrial revolution had its roots in Birmingham, England. Automation and the automobile industry took off in Detroit. The financial and publishing industries sprouted in New York City and London, and the digital age's biggest companies and thinkers are congregated in the urban areas of Silicon Valley. Most of the great ideas in our modern times have their roots in cities. "Cities," wrote Glaeser, "are our species' greatest invention."

––––

In 1472, when Leonardo da Vinci was twenty years old, the Italian essayist Benedetto Dei wrote that the city of Florence "has all of the fundamental things a city requires for perfection. First of all, it enjoys complete liberty; second, it has a large, rich, and elegantly dressed population; third, it has a river with clear, pure water, and mills within its walls; fourth, it rules over castles and towns, lands and people; fifth, it has a university, and both Greek and accounting are taught; sixth, it has masters in every art; seventh, it has banks and business agents all over the world." Okay, so maybe the elegantly dressed population and the teaching of Greek are a bit out of date. But Dei's list of what makes a city great holds up remarkably well nearly 550 years later.

In the 2018 book *Our Towns,* James and Deborah Fallows chronicled their travels all over the country visiting cities and towns and wrote about how they were flourishing with ideas and innovations and progress. Within the book, they came up with their own ideas for what makes a city great. Among them they included:

- pragmatic, not partisan, local governments
- public-private partnerships
- livable downtowns
- proximity to a research university
- good community colleges
- innovative schools
- openness to immigrants
- revived civic attractions, such as walking or biking paths or a repurposed industrial waterfront

It's an excellent and more modern list than Dei's. My own list for what makes for a great city would include all of the Fallowses' list and most of Dei's (learning Greek is nice but not necessary). In Chicago we also added and modified a few items: We created quality schools—not just innovative ones—that give everyone a chance. We reinvigorated our community colleges so that they are relevant to our graduates' careers. We created a diverse economy that's open to all. We worked on affordable housing. We upgraded our public mass transit systems in all parts of the city and committed to improving infrastructure in general. We improved the park and playground system in every neighborhood. We revitalized our neighborhood library system to be the best in the country. We addressed climate change and shared ideas with other cities. This is how you make cities places where you can live, work, and play.

I think what you'll find in the rest of this book is proof that many cities of today hit many, if not most, of these marks. And that's the reason for their rise, for their success, for the trust their inhabitants have in their leaders, and in their cities.

———

When the U.S. Constitution was ratified in 1789, there were almost 4 million people living in the country. That's the same number of people who live in Los Angeles today. New York City has more than double that number.

As our country has grown, so has our federal government, becoming perhaps too complex and poorly structured to handle the challenges of modern times. When an entity reaches the scale that our federal government has, it tends to fall back on systems, processes, and rules, which lead, inevitably, to a hierarchy of decision-makers who are further and further removed from the impacts of their decisions. Our congressmen and -women, our president, and even the members of the Supreme Court are squirreled away in Washington, D.C. That centralization makes them easier prey for special interests that don't represent—and in fact block—the wishes and desires of the vast majority (see the National Rifle Association). It makes the entire entity slow and sclerotic. This will be hard to change on a dime. Sectors of our federal government have become quasi-monopolies, and as Leo Linbeck, a lecturer at the Stanford Graduate School of Business, points out, "no monopoly has ever reformed itself from within."

That complexity and distance, that self-interest, that faceless-ness and monopolistic tendency of the federal government, has put up a wall between voters and their elected officials. When that happens, trust collapses back to the space where government is more manageable, real, and tangible. Where it affects lives in a real and measurable way and functions because it tackles issues, acts nimbly and with agility, faces the future, and does it all in an affirmative manner. City government must respond to 311 and 911 calls. Mayors must get potholes filled and garbage picked up. They have to deal with income disparities, educational gaps, effects of climate change, immigration, transportation, and public safety. They must build for a future that secures the city's competitiveness with an approach that brings everyone along.

This is why trust is now found in governments and institutions that are more immediate, intimate, and impactful—America's cities.

———

Much of the transformation we currently find ourselves in is because of the fact that we are in the early stages of a giant revolution that is affecting the entire globe. Like all revolutions, the digital revolution, which began to flourish in the 1990s and early 2000s, has its troubling aspects as well as its promising ones. Its attendant upheaval is one of the driving forces behind the decline of the nation-state and the rise of the nation city. Some of those most unsettled by it, represented by the populist movements in various countries, have effectively kidnapped parts of national governments. Others have embraced the fact that the digital revolution has made us at once more global and more local. Either way, the world is changing, whether we like it or not.

We've been here before. History, while by no means a perfect predictor of the future, does have a way of echoing itself. Our current era, as Philip Zelikow has pointed out, bears some striking similarities to the second industrial revolution, which took place at the end of the nineteenth century and the beginning of the twentieth, when the United States changed from a largely rural country to one that was mostly urban. That transition caused all sorts of challenges, most of which were found in cities—poor sanitation, poor intracity transportation, overcrowding in tenement housing, and inefficacy in delivering utilities. There were also epidemics, like typhus, which killed thousands in America, and Spanish flu, which killed hundreds of thousands. All of these issues were eventually dealt with, primarily on the local and not the federal level.

Back then, the main burden of innovation and adaptation took place on the local level. Public health, electrification, and even railroads were all spurred on locally, much of it in partnerships with businesses. The best of these innovations and ideas were shared and imitated around the country. The federal government helped back then mostly by partnering and spurring growth.

We are here again. The burden of spurring innovations and ideas, of finding solutions, has once again shifted to cities and local governments. The ideas and innovations are spreading horizontally and no longer vertically. Luckily, there are some incredible mayors, both in the U.S. and abroad, who are up to the task of carrying those burdens.

FIVE

The Prospects

Shortly after I was elected mayor of Chicago on February 22, 2011, I learned that Mayor Michael Bloomberg was coming to town for a dinner honoring our outgoing mayor, Richard M. Daley. I invited Mayor Bloomberg to have breakfast with me the morning after the event, and he accepted.

At the time Mayor Bloomberg was halfway through his third and final term as the mayor of New York City. He was in many ways the most prominent of the vanguard of mayors who pushed along the transformational role of cities in American life. He ran the administrative side of the city with aplomb, turning a $6 billion deficit when he took office into a $3 billion surplus by the time he left. That was no surprise, given his successful business background. But the most transformative part of his tenure as mayor was how he used "soft power." He got the private, civic, philanthropic, and university sectors to run at their highest potentials, all in service to the city. His influence—because of the bully pulpit and his ability to use his own resources in the biggest city in the country—was significant. This trend of civic, philanthropic higher education and municipal government is part of a new emerging paradigm.

Bloomberg was a fiscal conservative and a social progressive. He believed that the threat of global warming was real. He was the cofounder, with former Boston mayor Thomas Menino, of Mayors Against Illegal Guns, which morphed into the powerful lobbying group now known as Everytown for Gun Safety. He traveled abroad, demonstrating the global reach of mayors. He initiated some programs that were eventually replicated nationally—the listing of calorie counts in New York City restaurants was later copied by the state of California and then enacted as a law for major restaurant chains in the United States. He was also an inveterate adopter and adapter of the best ideas of others, such as instituting smoking bans (copying California), establishing a bike-sharing program (something the city of Copenhagen had popularized in the mid-1990s), and banning trans fats (originally done by Denmark in 2003). Again, because of his prominent position, his adoption of these initiatives—and his demonstration that they could be done in cities—was transformational.

He was a Democrat, and then a Republican, and then an Independent, and then a Democrat again. Some have faulted him for indecisiveness or opportunism or both. But what this mainly demonstrates to me is that party labels for mayors are largely meaningless.

I mentioned earlier the tech center that Bloomberg set up in New York City. In 2010 he ran a competition among global universities to establish such a center on Roosevelt Island. The idea came to fruition seven years later when Cornell Tech, a partnership between Cornell University and the Technion-Israel Institute for Technology, opened up a campus there. This idea,

I think, is a 12 on a scale of 1 to 10. Understanding the role of an engineering and tech center in the middle of a big city and the kinds of jobs and economic growth that come from it was a giant, forward-thinking leap. It pushed the impetus for much of our country's research and development in computer science, information technology, software, and artificial intelligence, for instance—which, by the way, used to be driven by the federal government but is no longer—right into the heart of a big city. This type of thing is emerging in cities all over the globe—these partnerships among local governments, universities, and philanthropies, which are stepping in where national governments have stepped back.

So I was excited to pick Bloomberg's brain that morning at breakfast. We met at the Four Seasons Hotel in Chicago and took a table in a back corner, out of sight of the rest of the diners. I told him right away that I would be spending some serious time and resources working on education—creating a new pre-K-to-college model—and transportation and corporate recruitment and other big projects in the coming months as I prepared to take office. But I had a question I wanted to start with: "What's the one thing I should know that I did not discuss or debate during the campaign?"

His answer was simple: The best way to get a city going in the right direction in a short amount of time was to focus on tourism.

"What?" I replied. Leading up to the election, I'd had six mayoral debates and countless editorial meetings with the media, and tourism had barely come up.

Bloomberg explained that focusing on increasing tourism is an effective and quick way to create a host of new jobs, especially for those people in the city who do not have a college education.

At this point, Chicago's unemployment rate was 10.9 percent. When I left office, it was 3.9 percent.

I went back to my office that day and told my staff, "I want to know everything about Chicago tourism."

What I eventually learned wasn't pretty. In the city we had three different tourism agencies that did not work well together. We had only three tourism offices in other cities. (Los Angeles had twenty.) Our convention center, McCormick Place, had fallen from its place as the number-one convention spot in the country to number five, well behind centers in Orlando, Las Vegas, and Atlanta. That the facility was immersed in a damaging labor dispute at the time did not help.

So we went to work. We consolidated the three city tourism agencies into one entity: Choose Chicago. We opened up new tourism offices all over the world. We improved our infrastructure and buffed up our hotels. We wooed events to the city, ranging from the NATO Conference to the Laver Cup tennis tournament to the NFL draft to the James Beard Awards Dinner. Just to name a few. Within seven years we went from 39 million tourists annually to 58 million, a 48 percent increase. McCormick Place has reclaimed the top spot in the country for business conventions. (On the labor dispute, I sat the carpenters and teamsters down and said, "Let's stop fighting over our shrinking pie and grow McCormick Place together." And they dropped their lawsuits and we did it together.) When the Obama Presidential Library is built on the South Side in the coming years, it will do for tourism what McCormick Place has done for the business traveler. The $17 billion tourism industry has created 22,000 new jobs and supports a total of 150,000 jobs.

Needless to say, that was a great piece of advice, and we executed it with laser-like focus.

Mayor Bloomberg was always generous when it came to helping out his fellow mayors. When he was in office, he held various mini-conferences with, say, twenty mayors at a time at one of his venues. These meetings turned out to be excellent opportunities for mayors to get together for a few days in a stress-free and off-the-record environment to talk about the issues we were facing and share ideas. Bloomberg has continued doing things like this since leaving office. He helped found the Compact of Mayors, which addresses the issue of climate change, and he's chaired the C40. Through his philanthropy he established the Bloomberg Harvard City Leadership Initiative, which provides mayors with tools to govern more effectively. He also founded What Works Cities, which focuses on the use of data for cities.

One thing Bloomberg *has* been indecisive about is the possibility of running for the presidency of the United States. He's flirted with the idea more than a few times. Former New York City mayor John Lindsay ran for the Democratic nomination in 1972. Rudy Giuliani made a halfhearted run for the Republican nomination in 2008. Bloomberg is not the only former or current mayor whose name has been mentioned as a potential presidential candidate someday.

What follows are some snapshots of a handful of mayors whose names have been bandied about as possible candidates. Some have already run for president. Some may run in the future. Some may run for Congress. And some may stay put in their cities until they're done with politics.

What's significant now is the sheer number of mayors who have become national figures, known for their vision and leadership. There's a simple reason for that: These days mayors are the most effective government officials in the country.

In the fall of 2018, Eric Garcetti, the mayor of Los Angeles, and I had dinner together with our wives at an Italian restaurant in Chicago. At the time Garcetti had been mentioned frequently as a possible Democratic presidential candidate, and during our dinner the topic came up. Though he didn't reveal anything to us about his possible political plans for the future, I did give him some words of advice—and caution.

"You're the mayor of such a vibrant city," I told him. "If you go to D.C., you'll just end up racking your brain for nothing."

Garcetti, ever nimble, immediately turned the tables and asked me if I was ever going to consider running for president.

"No way. I've been there," I said. "And this"—referring to being a mayor—"is better."

Garcetti and I were once almost coworkers. In 2010, Obama was looking to fill a position he'd deemed the "urban czar," someone who could tap into the incredible innovation, economic and cultural, that was bubbling up in cities around the country. Garcetti would have been perfect for the role. But he had other things in mind.

In 2013, Garcetti became the forty-second mayor of Los Angeles, the city's first Jewish mayor and only its second Mexican American mayor in more than a century. He was reelected in 2017 with a stunning 81 percent of the vote.

Garcetti is an excellent leader. He's created an innovative process of matching homeless veterans with homes, a program the federal government has been unable to do. He's twice raised Los Angeles's minimum wage. When he met with the crown prince of Saudi Arabia, he pressed him on human and women's rights and didn't just seek to do business like members of Trump's inner circle have done. He's been a particularly strong leader on three significant issues that face our nation these days: immigration, infrastructure, and climate change.

———

Los Angeles can make a strong case for being the modern-day Ellis Island. Sixty-three percent of the 4 million people in Los Angeles are either immigrants or the children of immigrants. Garcetti—like all good mayors and unlike many Republicans at the federal level—rightly views these immigrants as a strength and not a weakness. Our cities these days are entrepreneurial, and immigrants are a big part of the reason why. According to the Kauffman Foundation, immigrants are nearly twice as likely to start a new business as native-born Americans. They start nearly one third of all new businesses in the country (in Los Angeles, 61 percent of the businesses on the main streets were started by immigrants), employ nearly one out of every ten Americans in privately owned businesses, and generate $775 billion in revenues. Many of these businesses are small, the mom-and-pop shops that hold together any city in the world. But others aren't. The National Foundation for American Policy, a nonpartisan research group, says that immigrants founded forty-four of the eighty-seven American tech companies that are valued at $1 billion or above. Some of these folks are among the richest people in the world.

Garcetti, like everyone with a scintilla of conscience, was appalled by the Trump administration's policy of separating parents and children at the border and his mandate to Immigration and Customs Enforcement officers to round up immigrants already in the country and send them home without any due process. Los Angeles is a sanctuary city, of course, but Garcetti has taken things even further. He's focused his efforts not on fighting the mandates of the federal government but on maneuvering around them and doing the sensible thing of working to make the city's estimated 350,000 undocumented immigrants legal. "Here at the local level, where the rubber meets the road, we are carrying out what the federal government should be doing," he says.

Garcetti looked to one of the great democratic institutions for help: the library (the same institution, you'll remember, that I turned to for help in tutoring Chicago public school kids). Garcetti borrowed our idea and set up immigration centers in seventy-three libraries in Los Angeles, where the undocumented could go safely to get information on becoming a legal citizen, study for citizenship exams, or just ask questions of the librarians, who have all been trained as immigration assistants. Through this program, the city of Los Angeles has helped some 48,000 people with their immigration status. The federal government has made it more difficult for any immigrant to become documented. Garcetti and Los Angeles are working to right that wrong.

"Everyone belongs in American cities," says Garcetti. "Tolerance, diversity, and belonging reflect a moral position. It's also the embodiment of our country's principles. But we don't just take moral positions because they feel good. We're pro-immigrant here because we are pro-economy. But more than that, we are pro-family. We are a stronger city, and stronger country, when we keep all families together."

———

Bad traffic is, unfortunately, something that Los Angeles is known for. Its drivers spend an average of eighty-one hours per year stuck in traffic. This congestion affects so many things in a city—its health and livability. Garcetti knew he had to tackle the issue, and he knew he'd have to do it without any help from the federal government.

On the same night in November 2016 that Trump was elected president, the citizens of Los Angeles did a remarkable thing: They voted "yes" on what's known as Measure M, an enormous $120 billion, forty-year program championed by Garcetti that will fix their roads and freeways and build fifteen new rapid transit lines. To fund the project, they voted to impose a 1 percent sales tax on themselves.

Like me, Garcetti realized just how important his main airport is to his city and its vibrancy. To that end he got a $14 billion plan approved by the city council to update the terminals at Los Angeles International Airport and, for the first time ever, to provide public transportation to and from it. (Much of the funding will come from the airport's operating revenues.) The city will also be spending $2.5 billion on its port, which is the largest in the country, and another $5 billion upgrading the city's electricity and water supply systems. In all, Los Angeles's ambitious infrastructure plan is the largest in U.S. history. Garcetti tapped some federal money to get this done, but the bulk of the money (85 percent) will be generated by local taxes.

Like me, Garcetti became impatient as a lack of infrastructure spending—or even a plan—from the federal government threatened to cripple his city. So on a night when an antitax president won an election campaign based, at least in part, on what has turned out to be a false promise to rebuild the country, Garcetti and his citizens actually did something. (They weren't the only ones—Seattle and Atlanta also passed significant infrastructure propositions that night.) "Our voters, to their credit, basically said, 'The cavalry is not coming from D.C.,'" he says.

———

That infrastructure project will also benefit the environment, of course, by reducing emissions. "Cities are where it's at in terms of attacking climate change," says Garcetti. "They always have been, no matter who is in the Oval Office."

It's true. The federal government can enact environmental policies (or not enact—or even dismantle—regulations). States also exert some influence on the matter. But cities are where the action takes place. Cities are in control, for the most part, of the three main causes of the emissions that make our planet warmer—buildings and how they consume energy, the generation of power, and transportation networks and fuel. "The federal government can't stop me from buying electric cars for our fleet, or stop me from strengthening our building codes, or force me not to make our water and power utilities carbon-free," Garcetti says. "The power to do all of this rests in our cities."

In 2014, Garcetti, along with former Houston mayor Annise Parker and former Philadelphia mayor Michael Nutter, cofounded Climate Mayors, a group of 425 mayors focused on reducing greenhouse gas emissions. He's also a vice-chair of C40. In 2015, Obama announced a plan with China to cap emissions. In order to work around a Republican Congress, he left the job of working out the plan to cities. Garcetti stepped in and hosted the mayors of cities in the U.S. and China, and the cities made bilateral and trilateral deals to reach Obama's mandate.

Los Angeles is already the number-one solar-power-producing city in the country. By 2040, the city plans to make its entire bus fleet electric. The city has pledged to become carbon-neutral by 2050. Chicago has also set that goal, for 2040.

Los Angeles has already seen positive results from its work on climate change. In 2016, the last measurable year, the city reduced its emissions by 11 percent. "Working on climate change is simply pragmatic," says Garcetti. "Ask a firefighter in California if climate change is real."

It's also economically smart. The costs of inaction are growing: Sea walls in coastal cities like Los Angeles will be wildly expensive. Electricity costs are already skyrocketing as the earth warms. Extreme weather events such as forest fires cost tons of money to deal with. The benefits of action are readily apparent. Health-care costs go down when air pollution decreases. And cutting emissions also creates new jobs. In 2016 unemployment in the city fell by 24 percent, a figure helped along by the creation of 30,000 blue-collar green jobs (which, by the way, is nearly two thirds of the total number of coal jobs in the country).

———

Far too often we anoint a young politician as "the next great leader" in politics before said politician is ready or has done anything to deserve such hype. Every once in a while, though, there is a politician who does deserve that hype. One of those people is Pete Buttigieg, the thirty-seven-year-old mayor of South Bend, Indiana.

South Bend is not a big American city. It barely qualifies as a medium-sized one (the population is 102,000). But the quantity of people governed is not the way to measure the effectiveness of a mayor. It is all about the quality of his or her leadership.

Buttigieg was born in the city he governs. He's a Rhodes Scholar and former McKinsey consultant. He was first elected mayor of South Bend in 2012, becoming the youngest mayor of a U.S. city with at least 100,000 citizens. A year later, while serving as mayor, he was deployed to Afghanistan for seven months as a naval intelligence officer. In 2015, right after he announced his bid for reelection, he came out as a gay man in an op-ed. Four months later he won a second term as mayor with more than 80 percent of the vote.

South Bend is just ninety miles from Chicago (we draw a good number of graduates of the University of Notre Dame, which is in South Bend), so Mayor Buttigieg and I have met on a number of occasions. In the downtown area, you can't walk ninety feet without running into an alumnus. Mayor Buttigieg likes to describe the job of being mayor as "the hardest and most rewarding job in the world."

It's the hardest, he explains, because of the level of scrutiny and immediate accountability. "You can't offer alternative facts. If a road is in bad shape, you can't point to it and say, 'This is the greatest road in the history of roads.' People will call BS." He also points out that you're always on as a mayor. "There is no legislative session and then we all go home for a break," he says.

But the rewards, Buttigieg says, make it all worth it. "You can get things done. We can be nimble and try different ideas and see what works and what doesn't. And in a matter of a few years, you can literally see things actually working, people getting jobs and neighborhoods rising. And it's incredibly rewarding to see that."

During his tenure Buttigieg has seen a lot of the rewards. Since 2012 the unemployment rate in South Bend has been cut in half and neighborhoods have been reborn, thanks in large part to the transformation of the city under him. Among his successful initiatives was something he called 1,000 Houses in

1,000 Days, in which he pledged to repair or demolish that many buildings to revitalize South Bend. The city was very much in need of a restart when Buttigieg became mayor, full of unsightly and unsafe abandoned and vacant buildings. Both citizens and businesses overwhelmingly backed the initiative.

Buttigieg started the project by basically getting everyone who had a stake—businesses and civic institutions, citizens' groups, schools, the university, and government entities—in one room and telling them, "Let's get this done for each other." He established the deadline of 1,000 days in order to give the plan some needed urgency. It was a critical component. "As the composer Leonard Bernstein once said, 'In order to do something great, you need two things: a plan and not quite enough time,'" he says.

To add to the pressure and accountability, the city updated the progress of the plan for all to see on its website. "You could see how we fell behind in the middle of the project and then when we caught up," Buttigieg explains. "It was a healthy combination of pressure and the right kind of reward structure. This is one of the things missing in the federal government."

Another thing missing in the federal government: actually getting things done. 1,000 Houses in 1,000 Days was completed two months ahead of schedule.

In all, the project cost $10 million. To pay for it, Buttigieg reprogrammed some federal dollars that were earmarked for neighborhood stabilization and applied some of the money from the 2008 mortgage crisis settlement. Repurposing federal money is a critical skill for mayors to cultivate. Creativity from mayors happens on both the idea and the funding side. "There is no deficit spending in cities, no printing of money," he says. "By law I have to balance the budget every year. We spend down cash reserves some years and borrow money sometimes, but there's no cheating on whether you have enough money to do what you say you're going to do."

This project proceeded hand in hand with another one that was called Smart Streets, which aimed to make the downtown area more accessible and appealing by converting one-way streets into two-laners and then narrowing them (to slow down traffic), widening the sidewalks and making them more aesthetically pleasing (with tree plantings and decorative brickwork), and creating new bike paths. Some fifteen miles of streets were rejuvenated in one year, all done with $24 million in tax increment financing, or TIF, which is a subsidy that is paid back by future tax revenue from that project. Since the project was completed, there has been more than $90 million in private investment in the downtown area, including new hotels, retail stores, and restaurants.

One of Buttigieg's mandates is never to wait for the federal government to catch up. "We need to act locally and lead by example," he says. One way he has done this is with paid family leave (new moms and dads get up to six weeks of leave at full salary). "It's hard to believe that we are the only developed nation without it," he says. Buttigieg couldn't impose the measure on the private sector, but he did do it for the 1,000 public employees of the city, leading by example. "Now these folks can turn to their spouses and ask them when their places of work will do the same thing," he says. "We've challenged the rest of the community to catch up." (Five states and a handful of cities now also offer some sort of paid family leave.)

———

When Mitch Landrieu took office as the mayor of New Orleans in 2010, the city was a mess. Recovery from Hurricane Katrina was stalled and mired in red tape, City Hall was besieged by corruption, the city had a budget shortfall of $97 million out of the $463 million general fund, there were 40,000 blighted properties, and . . . well, more than 100,000 potholes on the city's streets needed filling. The latter seems perhaps benign in comparison with the other problems. But believe me, it's not.

"When I came into office, I did things that would make Scott Walker blush," says Landrieu with a laugh, referring to the slash-and-burn, union-hating former governor of Wisconsin. Landrieu immediately cut 22 percent out of the city's budget by figuring out and then laying out the city's core mission of delivering goods and services as efficiently as possible, and then basing every cutting decision on that. "I asked, What's its purpose? Does it help us? Can we afford it? Could it be done cheaper?"

One of the things he discovered was that having doctors and nurses on the payroll of the city's health department was inefficient and costing the city too much money for too little benefit. Landrieu backed an effort to transition to not-for-profit clinics in neighborhoods that needed them around the city, focusing on getting people preventive care, which saves lives and money. He staffed up these new places with the people who had once been on the city's payroll. In Chicago, we took our six community health-care clinics and partnered with Federally Qualified Health Centers, which saved us $14 million a year and improved the service and health care for the residents who depended on them.

He also got into a major battle with the city's firefighters' union. "Democratic mayors are not supposed to do that," Landrieu says. "And I had been the floor leader for the firefighters when I was in state government. I love them." Nevertheless, there was a problem with the way the firefighters' pension and retirement plans had been set up, and it was doing a disservice to the city and costing far too much money and threatening the retirement money of younger firefighters. They were putting too little in, making risky investments, and taking too much out. A twenty-year-old firefighter could work two days and then have three to four days off, have that same schedule for twenty years, and then retire with full pay. "It wasn't ideological. It was insane," says Landrieu. "I was a public steward and this system was unsustainable and it was my duty to fix it." It took years, with some nasty battles along the way, but Landrieu and the firefighters worked out a better deal, and in the process eventually saved the city hundreds of millions of dollars in liabilities and made the system solvent for the firefighters themselves.

Landrieu also consolidated the city boards and commissions, which had been little fiefdoms that rarely worked together, reducing their number by a third. He did away with an old procurement system and made it so no bidder in any contract could come to him—all bidding processes had to be public. "No more backroom deals," he says. "It's no longer based on who you know, but what you know."

There were also some antiquated systems within the city that were costly and unneeded. For instance, any new building in New Orleans had to have a boilermaker permit, even though no one used boilermakers anymore. Landrieu did away with that system and many other unnecessary building rules and regulations, many of which were rife with graft. In their place he instituted a one-stop shop for permitting, and many of the permits could be issued via the Internet. One of the results: The average time it took to construct a building in the city was reduced dramatically. Cutting unnecessary regulations is fairly simple, Landrieu says. You just identify the silly or antiquated regulation, go public with it, and then use the bully pulpit to hammer the message home with your constituents.

Cleaning up the budget and the corruption had a positive effect. Progress flowed from it. The city got its budget under control. The number of start-up businesses doubled during his tenure, from 2010 to 2018. The city's credit rating reached its highest point in its history. He improved the police department's response rate, which resulted in a 12 percent drop in armed robberies and brought the murder rate to its lowest since 1971. He developed a plan for more affordable housing. He worked with the state and federal governments to build an $800 million new VA hospital and a $1.1 billion university medical center. He reduced the blighted properties by half. And, oh yeah, he filled 360,000 potholes. The city still has some work left to do, but something more than a solid foundation has been laid.

But what I think was most impressive about Landrieu's tenure as mayor was the way he used his position, the "soft power" that mayors have at their disposal. In the spring of 2017 he made a remarkable speech about race that captured the attention of the nation. It was prompted by his decision to remove Confederate monuments from the city. That decision was a necessary one, he says. "The day-to-day functioning of a city, every little thing, is a big thing to a citizen if it affects them. It's also true that a city's aesthetics, its milieu, its spirit, the way she looks and feels and sees herself, is important." Landrieu says this spirit can be positively affected in small ways, like the flowers that my predecessor in Chicago was so adamant about having all over the city. Or it may be the way a city paints its bridges, or takes care of its municipal buildings. "That beauty is important," Landrieu says. "Those architectural designs, those colors, those parks all speak to the heart and soul of the city."

And those Confederate monuments, they, too, spoke to the heart and soul of his city. In his 2017 speech, Landrieu talked about how those monuments had been erected in large part to try to rewrite history, memorializing a fictionalized and sanitized Confederacy. He asked what it was like for an African American mother to try to explain to her daughter why a monument to Robert E. Lee was atop the beautiful city of New Orleans. "Do these monuments help her see a future with limitless potential?" Landrieu asked. "Have you ever thought that if that little girl's potential is limited, yours and mine are, too? . . . We can't walk away from the truth."

It wasn't easy—the removal of the monuments or the speech— and it wasn't welcomed by everyone, for sure. It was very unpopular locally, as he will tell you. But at that moment in time, as the federal government was stepping away from its responsibilities to enforce civil and voting rights, it was up to people like Landrieu to somehow find reconciliation. "This is what leaders have to do," he says. "People look to mayors to lead. We're the closest, most powerful elected official that's immediately accessible to the public, and that means sometimes you have to do things that are tough and make people uncomfortable, but things that you believe will get the city in a greater frame of mind and in a better position to win the future."

Our federal government seems incapable of healing our divisions no matter who is in charge, and indeed sometimes seems to foment them for political gain and purpose. The removal of Confederate statues is only one issue that divides our country, of course. "But I think all of those divisions we have belie a more realistic communion, which is found on the ground where people live," Landrieu says. "Those divisions and hatred don't play out face-to-face and in real time with most people. What's happening in our cities, in our streets, is so different from the conversation taking place on the federal level."

———

Of course, other mayors—both former and current—are mentioned as possible future presidential candidates (former San Antonio mayor Julián Castro is running in 2020). Mark my words: There will be many more in the coming presidential election cycles. Buttigieg, Booker, Sanders, Castro, Bloomberg, Garcetti, and Landrieu. Seven current and former mayors are either running or considering running for president. More mayors are running for president today than in the last one hundred years in both parties combined. That symbolizes the transformation that mayors and cities are having in the political system. Mayors have become the new governors, as it relates to producing presidential prospects. There are so many great mayors these days, many of whom would make great presidents. But they won't all run for that office, which is a good thing. We need them on the local level. We need them to continue to rejuvenate their respective cities and to keep doing their great and important work. "Mayors are some of the most talented political leaders these days," says Eric Beinhocker. "That shouldn't be surprising. If you're someone who wants to get things done and cares about the community and has compassion, then being a mayor is an attractive job, the opposite of being a congressman, who spends the day dialing for dollars and not getting anything done."

SIX

Leading Lights

There are literally thousands of mayors across the country who are transforming their respective cities and thus transforming the country from the ground up. Their progressive initiatives are working to make life better for their constituents. I could easily write another book that just highlighted the work that these mayors have done in only the last few years, as our federal government has been mired in ineffectiveness. Instead I want to talk in more detail about four people who serve as exemplars of the mayor model, mayors who have used technology, smarts, empathy, their position, and just plain common sense to tackle some of the biggest problems in the country. I want to start deep in the heart of bluegrass country.

———

"I'm a business guy who just happens to be mayor," says Greg Fischer, the sixty-one-year-old mayor of Louisville, who is now in his third term (his last because of term limits) leading a city that has flourished under his guidance.

Fischer spent his premayoral career working on solutions in the business world. At age twenty-five he coinvented, with his brother and father, an automated ice and beverage dispenser (they literally came up with the idea in a garage), which swiftly found a home in restaurants around the world. They eventually sold that business to the Manitowoc Company, and Fischer moved on to found bCatalyst, which became a mergers-and-acquisitions advisory firm. He sold that firm in 2010 and then ran for mayor in Louisville and won.

Given his background, it's no surprise that the hallmark of Fischer's tenure in Louisville has been modernizing the city based on the use of statistics, data, and branding. He has called on the people of Louisville to get involved in all the efforts of the city and the city government. "Citizenship is a participation sport," he says.

He was the first mayor in the country to create a city office of innovation. LouieLab, as he calls it, has a dedicated full-time workforce that concentrates on improving the performance of existing city services and constantly looking for ways to improve them or replace them with something better. LouieLab relies heavily on input from volunteer city residents. "We call them 'citizen scientists' because it sounds cooler," says Fischer. By combining LouieLab with Fischer's innovative use of data and statistics, called LouieStat, the city has done some remarkable things.

One part of Louisville was once known as Smoketown because of the ever-present industrial haze that hung over it. One of the legacies of that air pollution was a higher-than-average rate of asthma in the city. Through various real-time air tests taken throughout the city and thousands of volunteers who use asthma inhalers that are embedded with GPS trackers, Louisville has identified the most polluted neighborhoods. One way in which the city has acted on that information is to plant trees in those neighborhoods to help combat the air pollution (volunteers have helped plant an astounding 10,000 trees in the city).

Fischer also used data to transform the city's emergency response systems. A few months' worth of collected EMS data was quickly standardized. It not only improved ambulance turnaround time, it also saved the city $2 million. "We are constantly thinking about the city as an urban lab and asking how we can improve the human condition," Fischer says. "Government is supposed to improve the quality of life." It's a two-way street as well. Through the LouieLab, which has streamlined conduits for city-dwellers to share ideas, identify problems, and come up with solutions, Fischer has his city truly working for itself. Getting citizens involved in the problem-solving, he says, "has built trust, person to person, and people to government. And this is vitally important in a world where people are trying to tear down trust."

Fischer has also addressed the most important job a mayor has: education. One evening, after a series of all-day meetings at a gathering of the U.S. Conference of Mayors, Fischer and I went out for a drink. We sat and talked for hours about redesigning education. We swapped and shared ideas. We both knew that in order to make education truly effective, we had to start earlier and go longer in a child's educational life.

In late 2014 Fischer announced his own holistic education program, Cradle to Career, which focuses primarily on disadvantaged kids. "They weren't getting the social or mental or scholastic help they needed, and they were showing up at school at age six a full three years behind other kids developmentally," he says. "That's just not sustainable from a moral or economic or public safety standpoint."

Fischer addressed this by creating a program in which kids are given the opportunity for comprehensive free education—inside and outside the classroom—from pre-K to college. Though his program is similar to Chicago Star, he went about accomplishing it in a different way. "We asked the question, how do we wrap social services around these kids so our entire community is in effect raising them?" He focused on four different areas: kindergarten readiness, which increases the number of kids involved and focuses on the quality of care; kindergarten-through-twelfth-grade success, which streamlines the curriculum, making it more relevant to real-world jobs, and increases the number of extended learning opportunities; postsecondary education, which focuses on college readiness and more affordability and access; and work, which uses labor market data to assist people in finding jobs, trains students for regional employers, and boosts job training and the number of apprenticeships offered. Fischer invited every citizen in the city to get involved, from pediatricians to local businesses (which provided summer jobs for 6,200 kids in 2018). The funding for the kindergarten readiness program comes from a mix of local, state, and federal governments. The rest of the areas are funded by individual, corporate, and foundation donations. "We all had to pitch in," Fischer says.

This program, with the help of citizens, has already had a profound impact on the city's students. In just a few short years Louisville has moved from 10 percent below the national average in terms of kids going to college to 10 percent above it, according to Fischer.

What's also remarkable: Fischer did this on a shoestring budget. Instead of raising taxes to fund the educational programs, he cobbled together the efforts of existing entities to make it work.

The United Way, the Louisville public schools, the community colleges, and the local businesses all signed on to work on the plan together. Because of that collaboration and the money raised, the total cost to the city was a mere $12 million.

All of this—the use of data and statistics and the improved educational experience—has helped in the transformation of the city. Unemployment has dropped from 10 percent when Fischer took office to 4 percent now. Some 75,000 new jobs have been created (in a city of 750,000!), and 15,000 families have moved above the poverty line. Louisville's innovative partnership with nearby Lexington in something called the Bluegrass Economic Advancement Movement (BEAM), which works to increase global exports by and foreign investment in local companies, has been a huge success and a boon to the local economy.

Fischer has also pushed hard on the branding of his city, something he calls placemaking. The key for cities, Fischer says, is to ask themselves what they have that is authentic and that no one else has. "Our answer was bourbon," he says. "People go to Napa Valley for wine tourism. We wanted to create what we called bourbonism. As they say, 95 percent of the world's bourbon comes from Kentucky and the other 5 percent is counterfeit." The placemaking strategy is all part of a tourism industry that is thriving. Some 25 million people visit Louisville each year, generating $3.4 billion in revenue and sustaining 27,500 jobs. That tourism has led to an infrastructure boom in the city. Louisville now has $13 billion worth of projects either under way or in the pipeline, from refurbishing old bridges to building new hotels.

The above—and everything the city does and has done—is wrapped up in an unusual thing that I think is one of the most interesting ideas that Fischer has had: the idea of a city being compassionate. Fischer campaigned on compassion, which was somewhat of a risky gambit. First off, it's something that's hard to quantify, and most political strategists believe voters want hard numbers for everything. Second, it's an idea that's easily ridiculed as "soft." But Fischer was unmoved by either of these potential pitfalls. "I had consultants tell me not to run on compassion, that it wasn't strong, and that politicians all had to be tough guys," he says. "I don't believe that for one second."

According to Fischer, the notion of compassion means simply having respect for every citizen so that human potential can flourish. "As a country, we seem to have forgotten that we're all born with compassion, kindness, and love," he says. "At the city level, you can demonstrate how we can get back to that."

Promoting and fostering compassion relies much on the bully pulpit that mayors naturally have. The message and the tone from the top *do* have an impact. The idea works because it's being done on the local level, where citizens are not just numbers and statistics but people you see every day on the street, at meetings, and in coffee shops. But Fischer added some actionable components to it. He's encouraged the residents of Louisville to give a day to service during one week every year. So far, 235,000 people—which is more than a quarter of the population—have done so. "Imagine just for a moment if a quarter of the country did something like this," he says. Programs have been developed and implemented in the public schools to foster loving oneself and others, emotional health, and even breathing techniques to diffuse anger and violence. The health-care system and the police department also have programs for mindfulness and compassion.

Fischer says compassion is a concept that is no longer thought of as "soft." Instead it's become an integral part of living in Louisville. To Fischer, making a city smarter and making it more compassionate go hand in hand. "What we're trying to demonstrate in Louisville is that you can be compassionate and equitable, but you can also be innovative and entrepreneurial, and it's all part of a good, virtuous circle where everyone is in this together," he says. "Seeing it work has made me optimistic about the future."

———

In early June 2018, Mayor Sylvester Turner of Houston joined Eric Garcetti, Jonathan Rothschild (mayor of Tucson), and Tim Keller (mayor of Albuquerque) in writing a sharply worded, publicly released letter to the Trump administration demanding that it stop separating immigrant families at the border. "It was inhumane," Turner puts it, simply and correctly.

Later that month Turner went a step further. When the Trump administration announced that it was going to open a facility to house the migrant children (basically newborns to sixteen-year-olds) who had been separated from their parents at the border, Turner called a press conference at City Hall and stood on the stage with various Houston religious, nonprofit, and political leaders. He started the conference with a bang, getting right to the essence of the matter, declaring, "I've done my best to try to stay clear of the national dialogue on many issues. I've done my best to try to focus on the issues that confront the city of Houston . . . This one is different. There comes a time when Americans, when Houstonians, when Texans, have to say to those higher than ourselves: This is wrong."

That press conference put an end to the federal government's attempt to open a facility for migrant children in Houston. Turner used his bully pulpit masterfully to represent his city and stand up for what was right in the face of a national government that had taken a dark turn.

Turner grew up in a poor area of Houston called Acres Homes. His father died when he was thirteen. His mother worked as a hotel maid. Turner was the valedictorian of his high school, graduated magna cum laude from the University of Houston, and then got his JD from Harvard Law School. He practiced law for a few years before becoming a Texas state representative. In 2016 he was sworn in as the sixty-second mayor of the city of Houston.

Turner was challenged early on in his tenure when Hurricane Harvey smashed into Houston in the late summer of 2017. The city got enough rain to fill the Astrodome 3,200 times. Some 135,000 single-family homes were affected, as were 200,000 apartments. "People were hurting and needed assistance as soon as possible," says Turner. But the federal government was initially slow to react. Turner got the city response up and running almost immediately. Large city-owned trucks began to remove debris as soon as the floodwater had receded enough for them to travel the roads. But the city needed more help than that. So Turner began to travel to Washington, D.C., to plead Houston's case. Nothing much happened, he said, until he met with a Republican congressman. "I told him that many people affected by Harvey were Republicans and if he wanted to take responsibility for not responding to their needs, that was up to him," says Turner. The federal assistance for Houston came shortly thereafter.

Turner also faced down another crisis in his city, one that certainly doesn't make for dramatic headlines like a hurricane. But it is a vitally important issue, and one that affects most cities in the United States. That issue is pension liability.

In the U.S., local governments are now approaching $4 trillion in collective pension debt. Houston, when Turner became mayor in 2016, was responsible for a good chunk of that number, with $8.2 billion in pension liability. The city had not been able to get on top of the liability since 2001 and had been paying $1 million *a day* just in interest. "It was starting to crowd out everything else on the budget," says Turner. "It was taking money away from our green spaces, parks, and public safety."

Houston's pension budget is controlled by the state legislature, but Turner decided he didn't want to leave it up to them to figure it out. He wanted his city to do it. So he called together the three main unions—firefighters, police, and municipal workers. He outlined his plan: The city would reduce the unfunded liability (that is, the money owed to the city's employees by the city) by one third without raising taxes; the city would reduce the annual cost of the pensions by lowering the interest rates that were paid on them; there would be a mechanism in place to correct any dramatic spikes in the costs of the pensions in the future; the city would pay back the $1 billion it had borrowed over the years from the pension funds, and this would all be done on a thirty-year closed amortization schedule.

Turner then left it up to the three unions to tailor their own approaches within their respective groups to reach those goals. He and the unions met frequently in 2016. By the end of the year they had come to an agreement, a plan that they would present to the Texas state legislature.

With a bit of cajoling, Turner worked with the pension chairpeople in the state house of representatives and in the state senate. They carried it through their respective legislative bodies, and the Republican governor signed the bill in 2017.

Turner had used reason to fix a problem that had negatively affected his city for sixteen years. His solution was sensitive to the needs of his current and retired city employees. He convinced the unions to take a reasonable reduction in their retirement pay, but made sure that they remained fairly compensated for the work they had done and that they were paid back the money that the city had borrowed from their pension funds over the years. He crafted a plan that would remain affordable for a generation and would be resistant to future spikes in costs.

In the end Houston reduced its $8.2 billion pension liability by nearly $3 billion without raising any taxes, and it negotiated lower interest rates on the city's payments. Turner convinced the city employees to help out upfront by giving up some immediate benefits, to eventually gain more by reaping guaranteed benefits down the road. The inhabitants of the city also voted, by a margin of 70 to 30, to issue a $1 billion bond to pay back the pensions for the money borrowed.

In 2018, for the first time in seventeen years, the city paid its full annual cost for the pensions and still had money left over in the budget for other necessary things (green spaces, public safety, etc.). To be sure, not all cities will be able to replicate what Turner has done, for various reasons. But he's set up a template that can be learned from. More important: He's proven that it can be accomplished.

———

Tom Barrett is the forty-fourth mayor of Milwaukee. He was initially elected in 2004 and has since won three bids for reelection, each time capturing 70 percent or more of the vote. His constituents love him, maybe because he's a lot like them. He grew up in Milwaukee and put himself through law school by working on the assembly line at Harley-Davidson, a hometown company. He spent eight years in both houses of the state legislature and ten as a U.S. congressman. He's been innovative throughout his entire career. He's hard-nosed but kindhearted.

While Barrett "loved" his work in both the state and the federal legislative bodies, he says that being mayor has been his best job. "When I was in Congress and it snowed, I always said people would give me a pass because they'd think I was in D.C.," says Barrett. "Now, as mayor, if my own sidewalk isn't shoveled, people will notice and wonder what's going on. Being mayor is such a hands-on, real experience. It's unique among political offices."

Barrett describes the job as "very gritty." "I don't say that in a pejorative way. It's just descriptive," he says. "There's not a lot of theory. It's all about what works. And if it works, you keep doing it. If it doesn't, you stop and figure out a new way."

A good example of stopping and finding a new way to make something work happened with a program he called Earn and Learn, a summer jobs program for high schoolers. Initially he signed up local companies such as Harley-Davidson, Miller Brewing, and Milwaukee casinos, as well as some companies located outside the city, to offer jobs to Milwaukee high school kids. He thought the program would take off. While it had some success, it turned out that sixteen-year-olds had limited options when it came to working at casinos and motorcycle and beer companies, and that the jobs at companies outside the city were creating huge travel problems for the inner-city kids. Barrett could have been satisfied with the limited success of the program. But he decided to retool the entire thing instead. He and his team shifted focus to working with companies and foundations and individuals to offer jobs in the areas where these kids actually lived, jobs they could actually do. The program has soared since, and Barrett has been its biggest salesman, often cold-calling executives and foundation heads to ask for help. "I always start by asking them, 'What was your first job?'" he says. "Everyone can recall that, and everyone can recall how someone along the way gave them that break. And now they are in a position to do the same for someone else. I'm a big believer in momentum, both positive and negative. I think this program gives kids some real positive momentum in their lives."

Barrett also initiated a really fascinating program concerning children with absent fathers. Most broken-home programs focus solely on the children. Barrett's Fatherhood Initiative concentrates on the fathers, in conjunction with the support the city already provides for the children. Studies show that in disadvantaged families, fathers who are unwed or divorced rarely play a significant role in their children's lives. The idea behind Barrett's program is that these men can still play an important role in the lives of their children. "I just remember when I was a kid and I didn't make the football team and I was scared to tell my dad," says Barrett. "When I finally worked up the nerve and told him, he said, 'Oh, that's okay.' It was like a three-thousand-pound rock had been taken off my shoulders. He didn't really ever take me hunting or fishing or anything. But in that moment, he was there when I needed him. That's what fathers can do."

The program serves as a sort of support group for fathers who are struggling with money or feeling inadequate or estranged. It helps them try to find some connection with their children. Hundreds of men come together in the meetings to talk to professionals and to each other. "Many of these men feel so alone, but then they walk into these rooms and see all of these other men like them," says Barrett. In order to entice men to come to the meetings, he worked with the county to offer to waive the interest on their child support payments (but not the principal, so their families still get the same amount of money). "It's all very hands-on and practical," says Barrett. "The workshops include driver's license restoration programs and educational and job opportunities." The city chipped in $100,000 for the driver's license program, but other than that, the Fatherhood Initiative relies on volunteers and donations.

Barrett has also had Milwaukee act in areas where the federal government used to do the bulk of the work. One example is in the cleanup of old industrial sites. "We've stepped in and bought the properties and done the cleanup ourselves," he says. "We couldn't wait, because the private sector doesn't respond with investment until a site is cleaned up." Under Barrett, the city of Milwaukee has cleaned up an old Pabst Brewery site and an old rail yard, among other sites, to ready them for sale. Through a public-private partnership, the old Pabst Brewery is now a vibrant mixed-use site, with apartment and office buildings, arts facilities and hotels. The rail yard has become a twenty-four-acre park, with trails and bridges, that connects a lower-income neighborhood with the rest of the city.

Barrett has also been masterful at using the bully pulpit. A few years ago he challenged his citizens to walk 100 miles in 100 days. They responded by walking many more miles than that. "This is one of the ways you weave a community together and bond it and make it better," he says. After Barrett and I talked about how to further revive Great Lakes cities, he came up with a term for the area—the "Fresh Coast"—that I loved. " 'Rust belt' just has such negative connotations," he says. "Here we are on the shores of 20 percent of the world's freshwater supply. In reality what defines us is access to the Great Lakes and clean water. We need to rebrand our entire coast."

Barrett sold the rest of us Great Lakes mayors on an initiative that ended up being not just about marketing but about fighting for cleaner water and recreation. It was a brilliant piece of rebranding. And it's starting to work on tourists and, maybe more important, our inhabitants. I liked it from the get-go because it fit nicely with my congressional legislation, the Great Lakes Restoration Initiative.

———

When Nan Whaley assumed the mayor's office in Dayton, Ohio, in January 2014, her city was still reeling from the effects of the Great Recession. The region of 800,000 had shed 52,000 jobs. One of Dayton's flagship companies, NCR, had moved to Atlanta. A GM plant closed down. There was sequestration at Wright-Patterson Air Force Base. The federal government wasn't providing any relief. Moreover, Whaley says the state had cut Dayton's yearly general funds to $6 million from $13 million. "No one was going to come in and save us," says Whaley. "So we had to do it ourselves."

Whaley and her team decided that the way out of the mess was to go on the offensive and concentrate on remaking the downtown area. "We had to make it affordable and walkable, the kind of place where people wanted to live," she says. Whaley started by offering tax incentives to companies who moved into or built in the downtown core. It worked. Since Whaley took office, downtown Dayton has attracted $200 million in private investments, including renovation of the main library for $64 million and a $90 million restoration of what's known as the Dayton Arcade, a series of historical buildings that have become a mix of retail stores, offices, public space, and housing. She then moved to leverage the research labs of both the air force base and the University of Dayton to help transform the city's workforce. Manufacturing is still a mainstay, making up 18 percent of the city's jobs, but tech and research job numbers have skyrocketed. By 2017—the year Whaley ran for mayor unopposed and was reelected—Dayton's housing market was on the upswing, and the following year it set records for sales and volume, particularly for single-family homes and condominiums, which suggests an influx of younger buyers.

But it wasn't enough for Whaley just to attract young people. She had to incentivize them to stay. The best way to do that, she believed, was to improve the city's public school system. In 2016, Whaley proposed an income tax that would help schools and provide some money for infrastructure. The tax bill, which had broad support among the city's business community, passed by 12 points. Dayton is now in the process of making its pre-K universal and has robust programs for after school, summer learning, and internships within the local community. "To have business support for this in the state of Ohio was unheard of," says Whaley. "But our community knew if we are serious about the future, we have to pay serious attention to our future workforce." The remaking of Dayton is well under way.

Whaley has also been a very effective leader when it comes to our nation's opioid crisis. The federal government has (finally) taken some steps to address the issue, but it is still dragging its feet to a large degree. Whaley studied the issue when she was first elected, in 2014. What she discovered was that the opioid problem had become a full-fledged emergency in her region of Ohio. So she led with an emergency action: Her first step was to engage in harm reduction by offering needle exchanges. "We had to first try to save lives," she says. In 2017 the city exchanged 125,000 needles. That number has risen in recent years. And every addict who has come to exchange a needle has been offered—and oftentimes has accepted—professional help.

But the cost of that exchange program, and of the greater crisis and its ambulance and medical-care needs, grew exorbitant. So Whaley followed our lead and filed a lawsuit against the pharmaceutical companies. Dayton was the fourth city to join in and was in many ways the tipping point for momentum on the lawsuit. After Dayton, hundreds of other cities filed similar lawsuits. The current count of cities that have filed lawsuits is now around 700. (When I saw Whaley sometime later on, I joked with her that I wanted a retainer, since she followed our lead on the lawsuit.)

Outside of Dayton, Whaley has been quite the organizer. She has a way of bringing mayors together. She's long been an active member of the U.S. Conference of Mayors. When a colleague suggested she look into forming a similar body in Ohio, where cities routinely have to battle an unfriendly state legislature, she was all in on helping to create a unified voice. Whaley traveled to every single city hall in the state to pitch the idea. "It was superfun to do," she says. In 2016 she formally announced the formation of what's known as the Ohio Mayors Alliance, a coalition of mayors from the state's thirty biggest cities. It's worth noting that the alliance is bipartisan. One third of its mayors are Republican. Being a great mayor is pragmatic and never partisan.

On that note: All of the mayors in this section of this book happen to be Democrats. As for their Republican colleagues? Well, let's take a look.

SEVEN

The "Right" Mayors

What if I told you that there was a mayor in a coastal California city who, like Greg Fischer in Louisville, ran his election campaign on the concept of creating a kinder and more compassionate city and describes working on that issue as his "passion in life"? A mayor who went to the U.S.-Mexico border with Los Angeles mayor Eric Garcetti during the height of the 2018 family separation crisis and then cowrote with Garcetti an opinion piece for the *Los Angeles Times* that took Trump to task for separating children from their families, saying it "dehumanized" them? A mayor who went after Disneyland for its attempts to shirk its duties to the city it calls home?

You'd say this mayor is a pretty progressive Democrat, right?

Well, you'd be wrong.

Tom Tait was a two-time mayor of the city of Anaheim who was term-limited out in 2018. He has both a JD and an MBA, and he ran a civil engineering and architectural firm both before and during his time as mayor (he abstained from any municipal vote that had anything remotely to do with his company). He governed his city on two essential concepts: compassion and freedom.

Tait's idea of governing on a platform of compassion goes back to 2004, when he was a member of Anaheim's city council. He remembers seeing some strange posters, written in crayon, pop up around the city that year. Some of them read simply: "Make Kindness Contagious." After some research, Tait learned that the posters had been paid for by a man named Dr. Edward Jaievsky. Jaievsky's family had survived the Holocaust and had moved to Argentina and then to Anaheim. Jaievsky had become a holistic doctor and had six children. One of them, a girl named Natasha, died in a car accident at the age of six. Afterward Jaievsky found some crayon colorings she had made, and every one of them had to do with kindness; he decided to post them around the city to remember and honor her.

Tait sought out Jaievsky, and they met. Jaievsky, as a doctor, told Tait that he knew he could treat his patients with medicine but that the far better practice was to try to heal them from within, holistically.

That struck a chord with Tait. He realized that during his time with the city council, they had always treated problems that arose in Anaheim from the outside. They only dealt with the symptoms, like punishing criminals without trying to figure out what had led them to commit crimes in the first place. So when Tait decided to run for mayor, he believed he should run on a platform of healing from within—of treating the problem and not just the symptoms by promoting freedom and kindness. "I knew from my business background that a CEO can create a culture and a set of values," says Tait. "A mayor does the same thing."

Freedom and kindness, Tait believed, were closely linked. "Our Founding Fathers wrote about the need for liberty and an underlying need for virtue in society. All of the virtues in the world come together in an act of kindness." The way he saw it, kindness required participation. "You can sit on your couch and be nice and respectful," he says. "But you have to get up off your couch to do a kind act."

Spreading kindness and compassion throughout the city could, he believed, help with bullying problems in schools, with the loneliness and neglect that affect seniors, with crime and policing. "It creates resiliency and social capital," he says. "People are connected in neighborhoods by kind acts, and those kind acts promote more kindness. This makes us healthier and happier, and helps keep our neighborhoods safer and helps us prepare for emergencies."

Tait says he never received any pushback on the idea to his face, but he was told that some people believed it to be Pollyanna-ish and unserious. Some asked, too, just how the police force, for instance, was supposed to be kind. "I knew I'd be ridiculed and that some people would think I was silly, but I also knew it was the right thing to do," he says. As for the police force, he says, "Kindness means holding people accountable, too."

The platform had an actionable component. Tait charged the elementary school children in Anaheim to commit one million acts of kindness in one year. The kids rose to the challenge, exceeding the goal. (One child donated his entire $4,000 winnings from a game show to establishing a mariachi band at his school.)

Still, measuring the success of the initiative wasn't really the point. "We know things got better, just anecdotally," says Tait. "Whenever I was asked about how we measured the impact,

I would answer that I knew that just one act of kindness can change a life and turn everything around for a person. That would pretty much end the questions. Sometimes the most important things are the things we can't measure." The Dalai Lama heard about the idea and liked it so much that he invited Tait to Tibet. The Dalai Lama also came to Anaheim to celebrate his eightieth birthday.

Imagine for a moment if this type of leadership was displayed by those in charge of the federal government. Sure, it would be ridiculed by some, but the risk of ridicule would be far outweighed by the good that would come from it.

Compassion spills over into the debate about immigration, of course. Tait says he has constantly been dismayed by the federal government's response to immigration. "It's like Charlie Brown and the football," he says. Both sides of the political aisle, he feels, like to leave the issue unsettled because they both find it politically useful to do so. But on the ground level, action is needed. Anaheim is 75 percent nonwhite. In a city of over 350,000, some 70,000 people are believed to be undocumented. In the city's elementary schools, close to 40 percent of the kids or their parents are undocumented. "I represented everyone, whether they were documented or not," Tait says. "My primary duty was to keep people safe. You can't have people worried that someone will call the police on them. Many of our undocumented immigrants work in tourism and support our city. And there are a massive amount of kids for whom we need to provide hope and some sort of security. We let our elementary school kids know that we have no interest in their immigration status either way. We have an interest in their education."

In 2018, Tait and Garcetti traveled to the border together

and then cowrote the opinion piece to voice their frustration and horror, "because if the separation of kids from their families doesn't bother you, I don't know what does," says Tait. The duo also wanted to demonstrate that immigration, like many other issues, should be worked on in a bipartisan manner. "It's not a partisan issue. It's a human one," says Tait. "On the local level, we don't have the luxury of doing things that don't work. Garcetti and I may come from different broader philosophical ideas on the role of government, but at this level it's about getting things done and serving people. And there's not a lot of ideology in that."

During his tenure, Tait also frequently butted heads with Disney, the city's biggest company. When Disney opposed taxes that would help pay for city services, and when the company refused to pay its employees living wages, Tait fought back. "It wasn't easy to take on Disney, but I always did what I thought was in the best interest of the people of Anaheim and not the corporation," he says.

Tait's successor is a man named Harry Sidhu, an immigrant who became a U.S. citizen in 1979. He is a Sikh and is the first person of color to ever be elected mayor in Anaheim. He is also a Republican.

———

In the middle of 2018, I attended a meeting of mayors in Washington, D.C., and found myself sitting next to Bryan Barnett, the mayor of Rochester Hills, Michigan, a city twenty-five miles north of Detroit. Barnett is a Republican and represents a solidly Republican city. There is no way he would win a mayoral election in Chicago, and there is no way I would win an election in

Rochester Hills. But Barnett and I have more in common than it might seem to an outsider.

That day we talked about immigration and how the issue affects our respective cities (New York City mayor Bill de Blasio joined us for a portion of the conversation). Immigration—and the way it's being handled, or really mishandled, on the federal level—is a big concern for both of us. Barnett talked about how his community, though mainly wealthy and white, had the third largest Asian population in Michigan, the largest Albanian Catholic church outside of Albania, and the second largest mosque in metro Detroit. He told me about how he had put together a commission on diversity and inclusion, made up of business, faith, educational, and nonprofit leaders to "help foster diversity" in his city. He talked about how his local businesses were always looking for talent, and much of that talent came from overseas. In short, what he was describing was not too different from the way I've described Chicago: as a welcoming city. "If what I'm doing relative to immigration and diversity is creating economic opportunity and jobs, it's a core principle of the Republican Party," says Barnett. "How I get to that principle may be a bit different from people further right, but those things to me are creating self-sufficiency, and in order to achieve that you must have a system that works and gives everyone a chance."

Barnett was full-throated in his opposition to some of the Trump administration's immigration policies. "I don't feel like I have to march in step with what's coming out of Washington, D.C.," he says. I was impressed by Barnett (and I thought that if he kept talking like that, maybe he *could* run for mayor in Chicago!).

On the issue of climate change, too, Barnett has taken a different tack from many of his fellow Republicans on the federal level. And he's done it in a way that has appealed to his relatively conservative-leaning citizens. Rochester Hills, despite the high level of education achieved by the majority of its citizens, was the worst-performing city in the Midwest when it came to recycling. Barnett wanted to change that, so he started a recycling program that offered incentives—people could earn money, to keep or donate, by recycling. (A recycling truck measured their amount of recycled goods and then awarded points that could be used to buy goods or be given away.) Soon enough, Rochester Hills went from worst to first in the Midwest in recycling. The program has saved money and has raised hundreds of thousands of dollars for the local schools, where many city residents chose to donate their recycling proceeds. "For our part, we weren't going around talking about polar ice caps melting," says Barnett. "But we were talking about saving money and about raising money for schools. It was an economic argument and one that made sense to the people in our community."

Barnett has also done an excellent job of making Rochester Hills a great place to live, without any real help from the federal government. During and after the Great Recession, even relatively well-off cities like Rochester Hills had little money to spend on parks and infrastructure. "We were just trying to pay our policemen and firefighters," says Barnett. But he knew how important parks and open spaces are to a city's downtown area, in both an economic and a livability sense. In the middle of the city there were 130 acres of former industrial land, with hills and a river running right through it. Barnett wanted to turn the land into a giant park, but he couldn't pay for the construction, much less a design. So he hit on the idea of getting a design for free, with the hope that if people could actually *see* a vision for the park, they would pitch in with donations. He appealed to Lawrence Technological University, a local college, to do a design contest as a class project. "I just asked them to think of the most amazing thing they could, with no price tag," says Barnett. A few months later, the school presented its contest winner to Barnett and the city's climate commission. Barnett showed the plans to a local businessman, who loved them so much he wrote the city a $1 million check to get something started. Barnett leveraged that donation to get the rest of the needed money from nonprofits and state grants.

The park—complete with lakes and glow-in-the-dark pathways and a section for people with special needs—is now under construction. Innovation Hills, as it's named, will be an extraordinary place that will make Rochester Hills a healthier, happier, and better place to live. "We never would have gotten it done if we'd waited around for help," says Barnett.

Barnett, who won his third term in 2015 as a write-in candidate (the city charter limits mayors to two terms but says that anyone can run as a write-in candidate), says he looks at his job and the things he's done and is planning to do in the future through a pragmatic, nonpartisan lens. "There are folks in my party who are against government, but I think there is an appropriate role for it," he says. "I keep my team focused on constantly trying to add value to and improve the lives of the people in our community. I work for them. I don't work for the president or Congress." You just can't say something like this at the federal level.

———

Carmel, Indiana, is a small but growing city located outside of Indianapolis. If you look at the résumé and accomplishments of the city's Republican mayor, Jim Brainard, you'd think he was among the most progressive mayors in the country. He is the cochair of the Energy Independence and Climate Protection Task Force of the U.S. Conference of Mayors. President Obama appointed him to something called the Task Force on Climate Preparedness and Resilience. He's had a standing executive order since 2005 for his government to purchase hybrid and biofuel vehicles. He started a bike-sharing program in his city. Under his watch, hundreds of acres of parkland and green spaces have been created within the city limits. He is a big proponent of diversity and told his local newspaper, "When I study the history of our cities, I see that the most important advances take place when people of diverse backgrounds meet." He has created an Inter-faith Alliance that brings together leaders of different religious faiths, and he hosts an annual Iftar dinner for his city's Muslim population. In response to then-Indiana governor Mike Pence's 2015 "religious freedom" law, which discriminated against gays, Brainard and his city council (with a 7–0 vote) passed a law that made it illegal in their city to discriminate on the basis of sexual orientation, religious beliefs, race, or gender identity. Oh yeah, and he listens to National Public Radio in his office.

Brainard's smart, pragmatic, and progressive policies have been welcomed by Carmel. He is currently in his sixth term as the mayor of the city. (Note to Mayor Brainard: There's plenty of room for you in the Democratic Party.)

When Brainard goes on the road to promote his city, he starts his presentation with a slide of San Diego with blue waves crashing on its shore and one of Aspen with its snowcapped mountains. "We are not these places, we don't have this built-in attraction," he tells people in these meetings. "We are Carmel, Indiana. But what we do have is a city that provides a good quality of life, with a feeling of inclusiveness and community for everyone. People choose to live in Carmel because of the type of place it is."

More and more people have chosen Carmel over the years. The city has almost quadrupled in size, to 95,000, since Brainard became mayor (some of that growth came from rezoning, but much of it has been organic). The welcoming environment of the city is a big reason why. But so are the improvements that he's made to the downtown area, which have made the city more economically vibrant and livable.

Over the years Brainard has in effect created an entirely new downtown in Carmel, which includes a $175 million, 1,600-seat concert hall (designed by Washington, D.C., architect David Schwarz and paid for with a TIF), two theaters, a City Center, an Arts and Design District, and parkland, which he's increased from forty acres to well over one thousand.

The redevelopment was done through either TIFs or public-private partnerships (Brainard has stayed true to a part of his Republican roots—Carmel maintains the lowest tax rates in the state of Indiana). What Brainard is most famous for, though, is his innovative solution to the city's former congestion and pollution problems. In an idea he says he stole from a town in England, Brainard has installed more than one hundred roundabouts on his city's streets, which have replaced traditional traffic-light intersections.

The roundabout program has changed the city in a great way. It conserves gas and reduces air pollution because it does away with idling at red lights and the extra emissions that come from the accelerations at green lights. By taking out many of the city's traffic lights, Brainard says the city has conserved electricity and saved $300,000 in costs. The roundabouts have also saved lives, reducing driver-basis injury rates by 68 percent. "There will always be bad drivers, but the difference now is that we don't have people blowing through a red light at 50 miles per hour," he says. "Instead we have drivers going through roundabouts at 15 miles per hour." The roundabouts have also saved time, because they process traffic constantly, whereas intersections with lights are empty between every single light change. What was once a thirty-minute drive from the outskirts of town to the city core now takes fifteen minutes. According to Brainard, Carmel now has more roundabouts than any city in North America. The initiative won him first-place honors in the 2008 Mayor's Climate Protection Awards Program.

Brainard believes that inclusiveness and conservation were once traditionally Republican issues. On inclusiveness, he says, "Why should the government be telling people how to live their personal lives?" As for the environment, he points out that from Teddy Roosevelt through Nixon, Republican leaders once championed preservation. "This should be a nonpartisan issue," he says. "I've yet to find a Republican or Democrat who wants their family to drink dirty water or breathe dirty air. Our responsibility is to take care of the earth and leave it in better shape for future generations."

Like Bryan Barnett, Brainard frames these issues in a different manner for constituents who don't necessarily have progressive views. "I had a Tea Party type complain to me about the $1 million I spent on replacing our streetlights with LEDs [more environmentally friendly light-emitting diode bulbs]," says Brainard. "I told him to forget the environment for a minute and think about this: We are getting a 22 percent return on investment through lower electricity costs now. The guy's eyes opened wide. We can get to the same endpoint for different reasons with different people."

———

One day in 2006, Mick Cornett, the mayor of Oklahoma City, looked at himself in the mirror and did not like what he saw. "I'd become obese," he says. He wasn't the only one in his city. That same year a prominent men's fitness magazine named Oklahoma City the thirteenth fattest city in the country.

In the ensuing year Cornett lost forty-two pounds and found himself thinking a lot about the issue. "One of the things I realize is that people talk about exercise and smoking, but we really don't talk about obesity," he says. "I really didn't know how to talk about it, but I knew I wanted to start a discussion."

He hit upon the idea of an awareness campaign that challenged the people of Oklahoma City to lose weight. To kick off the campaign, he went to the zoo and held a press conference in front of the elephants to get the message across. He declared that he was putting the entire city on a diet, and wanted the population collectively to lose one million pounds. "I wanted it to be fun," he says. He enlisted local businesses to help out. The city's Taco Bell franchises all installed a life-sized cardboard cutout of him, along with a list of healthier menu items. Pastors talked to their congregations about it. A friend of his designed a website to track the city's progress.

The campaign exploded. Cornett went on *The Ellen DeGeneres Show* to talk about it. That same men's fitness magazine that had written about Oklahoma City's weight problem did a piece on the program. And within four years the city had met, and then exceeded, its goal, with more than 50,000 people signing on to lose weight.

By Cornett's own admission, there was nothing scientific

about the endeavor. They didn't actually measure the weight loss of individual citizens—it wasn't practical to do so. Also, it wasn't necessarily a weight-loss campaign. Much like Tait's compassion campaign, Cornett's efforts here were about raising awareness and social connectivity and getting people to really think about their health and the choices they make. And by that measure, it was a smashing success. "It demonstrated the influence that we mayors have," he says. "No other person in the city can put the citizens on a diet except for the mayor."

But much of what made Cornett's long tenure as the mayor of Oklahoma City such a success *could* be measured in concrete terms. He was the first mayor in Oklahoma City's history to win four terms, a fifteen-year run that began in 2004. Under Cornett, 100,000 new jobs were created in the city, 10,000 new businesses were created, and there were seven straight years of double-digit population growth. He balanced the city's budget *and* invested more than $2 billion in schools and infrastructure. He helped woo a National Basketball Association franchise to the city.

Cornett was born and raised in Oklahoma City, so he was there during some of the city's low moments in the past. For decades the city had no real identity, nothing unique or authentic about it. In 1991, United Airlines announced that it was going to build a new maintenance facility. Oklahoma City was one of many midwestern cities that vied for the plant. The city back then desperately needed jobs. The mayor at the time, Ron Norick, passed a sales tax that would help get the facility built and spent a year tirelessly wooing United Airlines executives, promising even more incentives. Oklahoma City had by far the best offer for the new facility, but it finished second to Indianapolis. The reason provided by the United Airlines executives for the snub was quite harsh: Their employees didn't want to live in Oklahoma City.

Then, in 1995, there was the horrific bombing of the Alfred P. Murrah Federal Building downtown, which, fairly or not, branded the city for years to come.

Norick, to his credit, knew the city needed to take some radical steps to change its identity, its economics, its livability. One of the most significant ways he did that was through something called Metro Area Projects Plans (MAPS), which are major capital improvement programs.

By the time Cornett took over as mayor, Oklahoma City had begun its rise. Cornett put that rise on steroids. In his first five years in office, the city added 72,000 jobs. It made it through the Great Recession just fine: During that time it had the second lowest rate of unemployment in the country for metropolitan areas of more than one million people, and it had one of the best rates of GDP growth among the country's major metro areas. He helped push through what was known as MAPS for Kids, a $700 million program started under his predecessor designed to renovate and rebuild schools in the city. In 2009 he devised his own MAPS program, called MAPS 3, which focused on improving the quality of life in the city. The $777 million program helped build a new convention center, a seventy-acre downtown park, a streetcar/transit system, biking and walking trails, and new wellness centers for seniors. The money came from a sales tax. The genius of the MAPS programs is that the taxes collected were not put into a general fund; instead they were put into a fund designated only for the project. When that project was done, the tax expired. This was a very creative way for a Republican mayor to get what could have been a reluctant populace to back a new tax. The MAPS template is such a sound one, particularly for small to medium-sized cities. More than thirty cities have done something similar in recent years, including New Haven, Connecticut; Mesa, Arizona; and Enid, Oklahoma.

Cornett didn't stop there. He wanted the city to elbow itself up in the world. In the early years of the century he began to travel the country to try to get people interested in investing in Oklahoma City. He found some resistance. "The bombing in 1995 still tarnished our city," he says. "I realized that we wouldn't be able to build an economy on sympathy. We needed to be proactive."

Cornett believed that one way to rebrand the city was to get a professional sports team. He wrangled meetings with the heads of the National Hockey League and the National Basketball Association, but neither league had a team available. But he'd begun to establish relationships. "Everyone knew we were hungry for a team," says Cornett.

Oklahoma City got its chance in 2005 when Hurricane Katrina ravaged the city of New Orleans. That city's NBA team ended up needing a temporary home, so Cornett furnished them with one. Oklahoma City's residents went nuts over their adopted team, demonstrating so much enthusiasm that the city popped to the top of the NBA's relocation list. In 2007 that chance came. A group of Oklahoma City businessmen bought the Seattle Supersonics and then moved the franchise home the following year.

The Oklahoma City Thunder has been a positive addition to the city's economy. (The team's arena was part of the original MAPS plan and is owned by the city.) The team brings in a couple million dollars every night there's a home game. But to Cornett, the real benefit of the team has been that it has made the city culturally relevant. "It's changed the perception of the city by our own citizens and the rest of the country," he says, and it's neatly tied together the efforts of his predecessors and himself in improving the city since it was spurned by United Airlines.

The net result of the MAPS programs and the NBA team and the strong economy has perpetuated itself in the city in a very positive way. "It's all helped the city attract smart young people. The jobs attracted them, and then they attracted the jobs," says Cornett. "And they're sticking around."

Cornett left office in April 2018. His successor was his former chief of staff, David Holt. Holt obviously learned a few things from his former boss about the use of the mayoral position for good. One of the first things he did after assuming office was to take down all of the pictures of old white mayors that were hanging in the mayor's conference room. He replaced them with pictures of young children from the city, representing the city's different ethnicities.

Holt is a Republican, too.

————

These mayors are not anomalies. They are the norm. This revolution is taking place in all cities, large, medium, and small, progressively run by folks from different political parties. Republican Kevin Faulconer in San Diego has repeatedly condemned Trump's attempts to build a border wall and has embraced a plan that requires his city to end its dependence on fossil fuels. Fellow Republican Francis Suarez, in Miami, calls himself nonpartisan and has railed against his national party's stance on immigration. He was also named to a Bill Gates–led commission on climate change.

Do I agree with everything these Republican mayors stand for? No. They are not RINOs (Republicans in name only). They still are, for the most part, fiscally and socially conservative. But they are nothing like their counterparts in the federal government, where the party has been rigidly antiprogressive. Each of them has developed local solutions to the challenges we are all experiencing. More importantly, they are initiating change without a federal partner. These Republican mayors have followed the mantra of Republican president Theodore Roosevelt, who once said of governance, "Be practical as well as generous in your ideals."

EIGHT

Chicago (Home Sweet Home)

When I took office in May 2011, Chicago was the only major city in the United States with a coal plant that was still in operation. Two of them, in fact: the Crawford and Fisk plants, located in Little Village and in Pilsen respectively. The residents of these neighborhoods had been advocating for more than a decade to get these plants shut down, staging protests, conducting letter-writing campaigns, and even unfurling a huge "Quit Coal" banner on the smoke-stacks. There were aesthetic reasons for getting rid of the plants, for sure: The smokestacks were ugly scars on the skyline. But more than that, there were health reasons. Both plants had hor-rific environmental compliance records, spewing barium com-pounds, hydrogen fluorides, mercury, and sulfuric acid into the surrounding areas. These two neighborhoods had some of the highest rates of asthma in the city, a condition that was affecting children in particular. According to a report from the National Research Council, the plants and their pollution accounted for more than $120 million in hidden health-care costs for nearby residents. And the Environmental Protection Agency found that they accounted for around 90 percent of the city's heat-trapping carbon emissions that came from industry.

The pleas from the residents of Little Village and Pilsen had gone unheard, though. Or maybe they'd been heard but ignored. These neighborhoods were poor and predominantly Hispanic, which is the most likely reason that nothing had ever been done. It was a stain on our city, in more ways than one.

When I was a child, I used to go on weekend rounds with my pediatrician father. He took all of us boys, individually at different times, throughout the city. I think he wanted us to be aware of the world, and maybe to make us realize how lucky we were and how we should work on behalf of those who were less fortunate. I remember seeing sick kids then, kids with asthma and horrible coughs. Seeing the children in Little Village and Pilsen reminded me of that. And it reminded me that everything I did as mayor of Chicago was about and for our children and their futures.

One of the first things I did when I became mayor was to demand a meeting with the chief executive of the California-based company that owned the two plants. In between my stint with the Clinton administration and becoming a U.S. congressman, I worked for a few years in the private sector. One of the places I worked was a mergers-and-acquisitions firm, and the one big deal I did there—involving the company Exelon—had to do with energy production. An even bigger influence on me was a natural gas bill that I introduced as a U.S. congressman. T. Boone Pickens, a billionaire who had invested in natural gas, met me in Chicago right after that bill was introduced and asked, "How does a city boy like you know about natural gas?"

Well, I knew just enough about the future of energy production in this country to realize that coal was quickly becoming a thing of the past, a remnant of the early twentieth century. (The Fisk plant had been built in 1903, and the Crawford plant had been built in 1925.) Natural gas production in our country would likely put these plants out of business sometime in the near future. But I didn't want to have to wait for that eventuality. The residents of Little Village and Pilsen had waited long enough.

I told this to the chief executive of the company that owned the plants, and then I laid out two options for him: He could let me take him to court to sue him to shut down his polluting plants, or he could proactively shut them down himself. I also told him that if he did not shut down the power plants, I, unlike my predecessor, would support the clean power ordinance in the city council, and this would cost him hundreds of millions of dollars in cleanup costs. In short, I said, he should change his calculations when it came to the clean power ordinance. I told him that if he chose to shutter the plants, I'd throw him a parade.

A few weeks later I got a call from the chief executive. His first words: "What color will the confetti be in the parade?" The battle had been going on for thirty years. We finished it in fourteen months, a little over a year after I took office. The city of Chicago's last coal plants were shut down for good in August 2012.

The symbolism and reality here were hard to ignore. Chicago, like all great modern cities, had finally moved on from its industrial polluting past. But this was a big deal to me for more reasons than that. Chicago is my hometown. Its people are my neighbors. The well-being of the residents of Little Village and Pilsen is, in a real way, the well-being of our city. The Pilsen neighborhood is now facing a new challenge: gentrification. The desirability of the neighborhood has changed significantly.

———

Every idea, every project, and every program we undertook during my time as mayor had a single abiding focus: to make the lives of the people of Chicago better than the day I became mayor and to leave them better prepared to make the most of their future. We didn't always succeed in that endeavor—there is no such thing as a political tenure without bumps and bruises and work left midstream. But our wins far outnumbered our losses, and I believe that our accomplishments—the things we completed and the things we initiated that will outlast my tenure and will stand the test of time—have helped ensure both a better present and a stronger future for Chicagoans. This is the key to what I'm talking about in this book, the thing that mayors and cities can do that the federal government cannot or will not.

I've told you about the O'Hare Airport expansion and the education reforms that culminated in the Star Scholarship program and universal early childhood education. These projects are all significant. They've deserved the recognition they've received. But we accomplished several less flashy but equally significant things that are worth mentioning because of their impact on Chicago; and in many ways, they are the answers to similar challenges other cities are facing. We didn't do all of these ourselves. In fact, most of them were a collective effort among our city government, citizens, businesses, nonprofits, universities, and various community groups.

———

Chicago's Metropolitan Statistical Area is the twenty-first largest economy in the world, and it's still growing. It's also the most diverse economy in the country—no single sector represents more than 12 percent of the economy. I always believed that one of my primary duties as mayor was to ensure that we continued to grow our economy in a healthy and inclusive manner.

Since the decline of the industrial city, universities and their graduates have become the number-one urban economic growth engine. Pittsburgh, once known as the Steel City, has been reborn as a city of innovation on the back of its twenty-nine colleges and universities, led by Carnegie Mellon. Boston has utilized its universities in the same way. We have, too. After Boston, Chicago has more institutions of higher learning than any American city. We also actively recruit graduates from other schools across the country, like the universities of Michigan, Wisconsin, and California. Every June, 140,000 college graduates come to Chicago to start their careers. Universities provide not only people with brains but a ready-made workforce, entrepreneurs who start new companies, and, most important, a culture of inclusion and a respect for diversity. Of the seven biggest cities in America, Chicago has the largest college-educated population (38.5 percent).

The universities and students in Chicago have helped the city rise as a place of innovation and ideas, with more than one hundred incubators and accelerators, and innovation hubs in major categories like software, health care, music and entertainment, food, and advanced manufacturing, representing the diversity of Chicago's economy. Our nonprofit digital start-up lab, 1871, now hosts more than five hundred early-stage companies, has a partnership with Google, and offers free workspace to our university students. It's ranked as one of the top start-up labs in the world. We revamped the Department of Innovation and Technology (for which we get pro bono help from local companies like Allstate) to help networking among the different entities.

This is where the density of cities is a true asset, where economic ideas can flourish among universities, labs, research institutions, and incubators and accelerators that are only feet and not miles apart. We've taken advantage of this brainpower by opening up the city's data for use by entrepreneurs and tech firms. This open sourcing benefits them, and it also helps us improve city services. The net result: Chicago is a tech center on the rise. In 2018 we had nearly $2 billion in start-up funding. A recent report from KPMG highlighted Chicago as one of the most innovative cities in the world and a rapidly rising technology hub, and we are number one in the country in return on venture capital. During my two terms, digital economy employment grew from 2 percent of Chicago's total to 11 percent. We also had the most digital start-ups led by women in the country. Another sign of working toward the inclusive growth we sought.

We have even bigger plans for the future. I mentioned Bloomberg's Roosevelt Island tech university hub earlier, the partnership between Cornell and the Technion-Israel Institute for Technology, called Cornell Tech. The genius of this center is that it has helped build an entirely new industry for New York City and thus has diversified it economically. New York has long been a center for the financial and design industries. The Roosevelt Island project has turned the city into a tech hub as well, and is responsible in large part for the city's incredible growth in tech jobs, which rose 56 percent from 2010 to 2017. The tech center is the reason Google moved 7,000 of its employees to New York, and why Facebook has 2,000 employees there, and why New York was chosen by IBM as the new headquarters for the company's Watson artificial intelligence headquarters. These tech jobs are important: They are less susceptible to downswings in the economy than other jobs. And no one ever said, "We have too many computer scientists, software engineers, and IT folks."

I liked Bloomberg's idea so much that we replicated it—we have put the University of Illinois together with Tel Aviv University to form what we call the Discovery Partners Institute, right in the heart of Chicago, which will formally open in a few years. I worked with Governor Rauner on this initiative. While we disagree on many things, especially school funding, he deserves credit for it. We then added additional research centers of excellence, including centers in biomedicine (at Northwestern University in Streeterville), a new computer science center (at UIC), and two new departments, one in quantum physics and the other in molecular engineering (at the University of Chicago). Some new initiatives in the city have already sprouted from this, including the building of what will be the world's largest supercomputer, which will focus on artificial intelligence. The Discovery Partners Institute and the rest, and all that flows from them, will further cement our place among the global tech leaders. I made it a practice to meet regularly with each university president to coordinate public investments in and around their new research centers. I saw these meetings in my office as essential to our economic growth, even more so than the corporate recruitments in which Chicago ranked first for six consecutive years.

It's worth mentioning here that not too long ago the federal government was the leader in our country's research and development projects. That baton has been passed down to cities, which are now our global incubators.

A city economy with a tech focus is dynamic—and attractive. I've mentioned all the companies that have relocated their headquarters to Chicago in recent years (ConAgra, Oscar Mayer, Kraft Heinz, and McDonald's among them). These companies all use technology, of course, and they all will benefit from Chicago's rise in that sector. (When Caterpillar moved its headquarters to just outside the Chicago city limits, it put its tech and digital headquarters within the city, employing twice as many people there as in its suburban headquarters.) The economic dynamism that's boosted by tech also helps the city pay its bills. Chicago's structural debt was $635 million when I took over in 2011. Thanks to our robust economy and disciplined fiscal approach, that's fallen to less than $90 million.

Of course, a dynamic, healthy economy must be inclusive and not just for the benefit of white-collar workers. It must work for everyone and help pull people out of the cycle of poverty. Our reforms in education are a big step in this direction, perhaps the biggest—just the reforms of the community colleges alone have led directly to a more inclusive economy and help bridge the diploma divide. But another thing we did has had a more immediate impact.

When I took office in 2011, Chicago's minimum wage was $8.25 per hour. Nationally there has long been a debate about raising the minimum wage, with some discussion of the possible risks, especially when it comes to how it could affect small businesses and entrepreneurs. Our research, conducted for almost three years, indicated that the potential benefits of a higher minimum wage far outweighed any potential negatives. So at the end of 2014 we passed an ordinance that kicked off a gradual rise in the minimum wage within the city. The following year, the minimum wage rose to $10 an hour. By 2019 it was $13 an hour. After that it will correspond annually to the Consumer Price Index, so it never falls behind inflation.

The federal minimum wage, which hasn't increased a cent since I was in the U.S. Congress in 2009, is $7.25.

Chicago is among some forty cities that have raised minimum wages in the last few years. It's a great example of how cities have led the way in a manner in which the federal government cannot and will not. The national poverty rate fell steadily from 2011, when it was 15 percent, to 2017, when it was 12.3 percent. There are those within the federal government who like to take credit for this falling rate. In reality they have done very little to combat poverty. The big drop in poverty rates began in 2014, when the national economy was growing at a modest pace. Though other factors have been involved, for sure, one of the main drivers is the fact that so many cities have increased their minimum-wage rates. The gradual raise of the rate in Chicago has lifted more than 130,000 people out of poverty. Almost half of those people were children. Our drop in poverty has been much faster than the state of Illinois's, which did not raise the minimum wage until recently. This is no coincidence.

Because of my work with Presidents Clinton and Obama, I knew the minimum wage was not enough to achieve the goal that if you work, you do not raise your child in poverty. As a key complement to the minimum wage, we pushed the state to expand the earned income tax credit in 2012, and then Chicago reformed it. We started a pilot program in which people could receive their earned income tax credit on a quarterly basis instead of annually. That way, working families can pay bills on time and better plan for the future. We worked with the Center for Economic Progress, a nonprofit that offers free tax preparation services to low-income Chicago families, to study the pilot. The study showed that families which received the EITC quarterly had improved their financial stability. The quarterly payment enabled families to stay out of the claws of the payday loan business.

Economic growth is good, especially when it works for everyone. But another one of the primary jobs of a mayor is to be a steward, to carefully weigh the costs and benefits of the manner in which money is spent and the ways in which subsidies and tax breaks are doled out. There are times, of course, when some corporate tax breaks make sense. Sometimes even an elimination of a tax is a good idea—we did away with the head tax in Chicago, which put a $4-per-employee tax on employers with more than fifty full-time workers. Breaks and eliminations in taxes can spur building and relocation and thus help the economy. There are other times, though, when a mayor must draw a line and say no.

Professional sports teams, particularly in the world's biggest sports leagues, are great for cities (just ask former Oklahoma City mayor Mick Cornett). They can bond a city together in ways that other things cannot. I love the Cubs, the Bears, the Black- hawks, the Bulls, the Sky, and the Fire (I even respect the White Sox, enough that I attended one of the World Series games!). I remember the great 1985 Bears team and how the city rallied around them. I remember the 2016 Cubs season and how the entire city held its breath—and then exhaled—when they finally broke the Curse of the Billy Goat.

But I'm not blinded by that fandom. What I am not a fan of is professional sports franchises and their wealthy owners tak- ing advantage of the goodwill of their city's residents. You see this all the time when it comes to the use of public money to fund stadiums and arenas. More often than not, doing this is not in the best interest of the taxpayers, who are providing, in effect, huge subsidies and tax breaks for wealthy owners who do not need them. That money can be used elsewhere, for schools, infrastructure, or the police and fire departments. Sports teams have gotten away with getting huge subsidies from cities because of the goodwill they generate and the pervading myth that the business they will generate will pay back the city in spades. More often than not, that just doesn't happen.

I ran into this problem in 2012 with the Ricketts family, who own the Chicago Cubs. They wanted $200 million in taxpayer money and subsidies to do some work on Wrigley Field and to build out the area around it. Like I said, I am a Cubs fan. I live half a mile north of Wrigley Field. I want them to do well. But the Ricketts are very well off, and we are a city on a tight budget. There was no way I was going to tap taxpayer funds to help them. As I told the *Chicago Tribune* in 2013, "When I first started this discussion, the Cubs wanted 200 million in taxpayer dollars. I said no. Then they said we'd like $150 million, and I said no. Then they asked whether they could have $100 million in taxpayer subsidies, and I said no. Then they asked about $55 million in taxpayer subsidies, and I said no. The good news is, after 15 months they heard the word 'No.'"

I don't blame the Ricketts for asking for money, even though old man Ricketts said I did not share their "values." That's what good businesspeople do. Plenty of big cities have unwisely done that type of thing for a professional sports team in the past (though to be sure, the cost-benefit analysis can be different for medium to small cities when it comes to subsidies). But I wasn't going to budge, because it was not in the best interest of the people of Chicago.

And guess what? Just a few years later the Ricketts family paid for the entire upgrade themselves, and they're making out just fine. As is the team, and the surrounding neighborhood.

I ran into a similar situation with the United Center, the

arena where the Bulls and Blackhawks play (the two teams operate the arena together). The arena had a significant property-tax break that was set to expire in 2016. I refused to extend it, for the same reasons that I didn't want to give the Cubs any more taxpayer money: The owners could afford it, and the city needed the money for other investments. Rocky Wirtz, the owner of the Blackhawks, threatened to cancel his plans to put the hockey team's new training facility in the city as an act of retribution for not extending the tax break. I turned up the heat on him a bit. The Blackhawks' new downtown training facility is really beautiful.

Sports teams, by the way, aren't the only entities looking for handouts. When Amazon first chose New York City as one of the locations for its second headquarters, it appeared to fit right into the narrative of the city's evolution into a tech hub. The company would be a perfect complement to the Roosevelt Island center and Google's and Facebook's offices. Then Amazon pulled out of the deal, unhappy with the resistance it had encountered from some New Yorkers, who themselves were unhappy with the nearly $3 billion in tax breaks and subsidies that the city had pledged to provide to Amazon.

Many believed that losing Amazon—and its promised 25,000 jobs—was a huge loss for the city. I disagree. While it would have been great to have the company and the jobs, the entire thing got off on the wrong track. Big cities, especially New York, which is in dire need of infrastructure repair, should not be offering tax breaks and subsidies to companies that have $1 trillion in market cap. It should be focused on its public works, like the subway system that serves the area Amazon was planning to relocate to. Then everyone wins.

There has been a bit of a demonization of public works in the last few decades, which has coincided with the demonization of the government in general. But public works are vital. And when they work, the private sector thrives; companies all rely on mass transit and airports, for instance. A city that improves its infrastructure, its education, its research facilities, and its protections (of things like the environment) will attract businesses and employees without having to dole out corporate welfare. These key public investments set the foundation for private sector growth. That's the right public/private partnership, as opposed to selling public sector assets for private sector gain.

———

Stadiums and subsidies and tax breaks are all part of a greater fabric at the very center of a city's being: urban policy. One of the great myths that's been perpetuated by the federal government, really from the Great Society forward, is that the term "urban policy" is just about housing. It's not.

Our new global, city-led world demands a rethinking of the term "urban policy." Housing is a very important part of it, to be sure. But what urban policy really is about, I think, is neighborhoods and community-building. It's not housing by itself. It's housing with transit, playgrounds and parks, libraries and schools, all of which provide the private sector with the incentive to open restaurants, grocery stores, and coffee shops—all of these offer sustainable, permanent jobs. It's also our museums, theaters, and all of the other things that have made Chicago such a magical place for me since I was a kid zipping around the city on the L. Urban policy is about strengthening and rejuvenating our sense of community and our neighborhoods. Housing without the other essential components that make up a neighborhood is merely housing isolated from all the other things that make a neighborhood work.

Public-private partnerships are key to building communities. So are initiatives that come directly from the private and nonprofit sectors. These kinds of partnerships—residents working for other residents—are so vital to the overall health of a city. They supplement and amplify the work that a good city government is already doing—many times growing from an initial public investment—and help fill in the cracks that the city government is unable to reach. These types of collaborative efforts are increasing in our cities every year. We're all in this together as a city.

In Chicago we now have more than a dozen community investment organizations that work in our neighborhoods, providing banking services, lending, and equity investing. One of the biggest and most effective community investment organizations is a partnership among the Chicago Community Trust, the John D. and Catherine T. MacArthur Foundation, and Calvert Impact Capital. The entity, known as Benefit Chicago, digs deep into the community, helping citizens find adequate medical care and providing loans for affordable rental housing and for small businesses and entrepreneurs.

Still, the majority of services delivered in a city come from the local government. We've done several things, citywide, to enhance the sense of community. Every year we provide free cultural events—1,200 of them, to be exact—ranging from concerts to a midnight circus, from Joffrey Ballet performances to Shakespeare in the Park, from walking tours to ice-skating. We call it Night Out in the Parks, and it has run for six consecutive years without any incidents.

On a more granular level, we've invested in housing in our

neighborhoods, for sure. But it's about so much more than just housing when it comes to healthy, thriving neighborhoods and communities. I want to talk a bit about three neighborhoods on the South Side, which have historically struggled with crime and poverty and much more. To me, they illustrate a template for how neighborhoods and communities can be reborn, how public investments can spur private investments and local job growth. They also illustrate what urban policy really is or needs to become today, if everyone is to have a shot at a dynamic city.

Washington Park, on the South Side, was traditionally a neighborhood with a lot of public housing, chronic crime problems, and little retail or commercial life. Several years ago we, along with a great entrepreneur, Kamau Murray, announced plans for a new $17 million facility for an organization called XS Tennis on the old Robert Taylor Homes site. It opened in 2018, and along with offering free lessons for 2,000 local public school kids (a number that will double in the coming years), the facility contains centers for both mentoring and academic help. When we hosted the Laver Cup tennis tournament in 2018, I insisted that the pros, including Roger Federer and Novak Djokovic, do some practice sessions in Washington Park. In no small way the facility has connected the Washington Park neighborhood to the rest of the city. The tennis center, the only black-owned facility of its kind and size in the country, is the anchor of a revitalized neighborhood and community and an investment that has borne fruit. Since the announcement of the plans for the facility, the neighborhood has added new mixed housing, a nightclub, new restaurants, a data center, and a refurbished L station (designed by the artist Nick Cave). Crime has gone down. The population, high school graduation rates, and employment have all risen. All these data points have reversed decades of decline.

In Bronzeville, another South Side neighborhood, we built a new train station, a new arts and recreation center, and a new school, and we rehabbed a library and four new bridges over the railroad tracks, which for the first time in decades connected Bronzeville residents to the lakefront. Those public investments led to private investments, like the opening of new art galleries, restaurants, coffee shops, and the brand-new Mariano's grocery store on an old public housing high-rise site. Housing values, graduation rates, population, and employment are all up, and crime is down.

That a centerpiece of Bronzeville's revival has to do with restaurants and grocery stores was no accident. When I took office, some 400,000 Chicagoans did not live within a mile of stores that offered fresh fruits and vegetables and meat. We knew we needed to do something about these food deserts. So we decided to make food a significant piece of the economic growth in Chicago. We tackled the issue from the macro to the micro level. I went out and recruited the James Beard Awards Dinner from New York City. I recruited ConAgra from Omaha, ADM from Decatur, McDonald's from Oak Brook, and Kraft Heinz from the suburbs as well, among other food companies, all of which relocated their international headquarters to the city. Then we convened a conference for the major grocers in Chicago. I made them a deal: If they opened a new grocery store in one of the neighborhoods that was a food desert—even if it was bundled with, say, three other stores in other parts of the city—we'd fast-track their permit applications, saving time and money. (We made a significant dent in the food desert population, but so much more work needs to be done.) And then we opened an entrepreneur-focused shared kitchen in Garfield Park on the West Side of the city, called the Hatchery, where food and grocery-product entrepreneurs could come together to share ideas and resources, and connect with the city's grocers to sell their new products in stores in the food deserts and beyond. We also rewrote our urban farming policy to copy Milwaukee's. This resulted in a dramatic increase in urban farms on former industrial sites in the city. From the international (James Beard) to the small neighborhood entrepreneur (like Justice of the Pie), we now have Chicago covered with the robust economic growth engine that is food.

Woodlawn, once a neighborhood riddled with gang violence, will be near the future home of the Obama Presidential Library. In 2018 we cut a ribbon at a new Jewel grocery store there. That sounds inconsequential, right? It's less so when you consider the fact that it is the first real grocery store, with a pharmacy and healthy food options, that has opened in Woodlawn in the last forty-seven years, eliminating another food desert on the South Side of Chicago. The *Chicago Tribune* has highlighted the rebirth of Woodlawn, symbolized by this grocery store. We also built a new school, and four new retail stores and a bakery have also opened recently, with the help of our Neighborhood Opportunity Fund. There is a new MetroSquash facility down the block, which provides opportunities to learn and play squash along with mentoring and academic help. This facility is an anchor, like XS Tennis in Washington Park and Ellis Park in Bronzeville. The University of Chicago has built some student housing there, and we've built some mixed-income housing across the street. The population is up. Crime is down. Public and private investments have worked in concert and boosted each other. This is how you form the solid building blocks that create a neighborhood and a community. These three neighborhoods are examples of the "new urban policy," as opposed to the standalone housing of yesterday.

Let me take a moment to talk a little more about these neighborhoods. In our cities, they are as vital as the business centers,
and should be treated as such. I knew that, during my tenure, I
had to figure out a way to make the neighborhoods grow and prosper along with the great growth of our business centers. What I
hit upon was something I called the Neighborhood Opportunity
Fund, which generated revenues from downtown investments
that would be kicked back to neighborhoods not served by banks,
so they could invest in coffee shops, retail stores, and other cultural and commercial enterprises. The idea was that when, say,
McDonald's moved its corporate headquarters back to Chicago,
they would get additional height and density. The company and
developer in turn would donate a percentage of the project to the
Neighborhood Opportunity Fund. When we planned the fund,
we thought we'd get $20 million over two years. We're now on
track to raise close to $170 million, with about 1,700 businesses
on the South and West sides receiving between $100,000 and
$1 million in grants. Think about this: Our federal block grant
is only $70 million a year. The Neighborhood Opportunity Fund
is only three years old and is generating as much as a key federal
urban program, if not more. The idea was that when a business
center succeeds, it sparks neighborhood, retail, and commercial
success as well. This, I believe, not only helps mitigate the divide
between the downtown area and struggling neighborhoods, it
also helps work on the greater problem of income inequality. The
Neighborhood Opportunity Fund has succeeded beyond our
expectations. The Urban Institute praised the program for its
innovation in sustainable growth, and recommended that other
cities replicate it; and they are.

In addition to our Neighborhood Opportunity Fund, we
required all developers to list all minority contractors on pri-

vate work prior to a vote by the Planning Commission. This public information has dramatically changed how developers now work, and helps the city achieve its equitable goals of inclusion. Trust me, no developer wants to go in front of the Planning Commission with zero minority participation in their projects.

Every mayor in one way or another has faced the criticism of a tale of two cities. I don't buy that dichotomy. Cities today are a tale of two investments: For years one part received investment; one part was disinvested in. The neighborhood opportunity fund, the new urban policy, a food desert strategy, and modernized mass transit are all part of a one city one future agenda. No great city has a hollowed-out core. On the other hand, no great city has decaying neighborhoods. Turning one part of a city against another assures the whole city loses.

What Washington Park, Woodlawn, and Bronzeville all have in common is that coordinated investments in housing, transportation, schools, libraries, and recreational facilities have spurred investments in new grocery stores, coffee shops, restaurants, and community art centers—a sustainable economic model that moves beyond urban policy as merely housing policy. It is also a more holistic approach to struggling neighborhoods. Rather than spreading the peanut butter too thin, a housing project here, a train station over there, it concentrates your investments to a single neighborhood. Chicago has succeeded in reversing decades of white flight, and has vibrant and growing Hispanic and Asian communities. For decades, however, it has been losing African American families to the suburbs. Bronzeville, Woodlawn, and Washington Park show a new way forward for all of us.

———

One of the most important building blocks we installed in Woodlawn, though, was a modernized L station.

Mass transit is the lifeblood of any city, and good mass transit is a sign of a healthy, vibrant city. As former Bogotá mayor Enrique Peñalosa once said, "An advanced city is not one where poor people use cars, but one where rich residents use public transport." People need to get around a city, for work and for play, in a swift and safe manner. Mass transit helps reduce congestion and pollution. Most important, though, a good mass transit system that interconnects a city—its neighborhoods, business areas, recreational areas, airports—is a literal vehicle for wealth creation. A train station in a neighborhood like Woodlawn spurs development. It connects workers with economic centers (the efficacy of the L is a big reason that companies and workers have come to Chicago). Studies show that access to mass transit results in better jobs and opportunity, and it is a significant factor in increasing the odds of escaping poverty. Cities that do not have effective modes of mass transportation—and cities that have subways that are in a state of disrepair—risk stunting their progress.

Starting in 2011, we embarked on an $8.5 billion modernization of the L, which is the second busiest mass transit system in the country. Four of the seven lines are already being completely rebuilt. We are in the process of replacing old cars with new ones. By 2019 we had forty stations that were either brand-new or reconstructed from top to bottom, with new elevators, escalators, and even artwork from Theaster Gates, Nick Cave, and Hebru Brantley (art tours are now offered at some of our stations). We have 4G wireless service throughout the system (riders can use Apple Pay for fares; we were among the first transit systems in the world to take this step), and we've begun work on the Blue Line branch that connects downtown with O'Hare, which will shave ten minutes off that trip. We also completely rebuilt the Red Line on the South Side as our first significant investment. This is the largest infrastructure project the South Side has seen in nearly forty years.

Our most ambitious project has been the modernization of the Red and Purple Lines. Modernization of train lines in big old cities can be extremely difficult—one only need look at the snail's pace of the modernization of the Second Avenue line in New York, which began in 1972, was halted, began again in 2007, and has just three lines (and two miles of track) to show for it so far. *The New York Times* wrote a story detailing "What the MTA Can Learn from the CTA's Modernization." The *Washington Post* did the same for the Metro in D.C. Our Red and Purple Lines, built in 1924, had been decaying for decades and constantly needed repairs, which gummed up the entire system. One of the main intersections dated back to 1907, when Theodore Roosevelt was president. The Red Line in particular is an important piece of the L. It connects some of the most densely populated neighborhoods in the entire country and subsequently has the most riders. The fact that ridership on this line is expected to increase exponentially in the coming years made its revitalization a priority.

So we knew these lines needed modernizing. The question then became how we would pay for it. That was the tricky part. The state and federal governments had not passed a transportation bill in many years, and there was no prospect of their doing it soon. We had to get creative. The federal government wasn't exactly reaching out to help, even though we knew it had the funds somewhere. So we decided to try to create the money ourselves.

I had my staff reach out to Dick Durbin, the senior U.S. senator from Illinois. With his help, we found, and then applied for, and then received a federal grant from what's known as the Core Capacity Fund, which was a President Obama initiative. I had encouraged President Obama to create and fund it in his budget, and we were the first applicants. (Funny how that happened.) We also found some money in a federal program called Congestion Mitigation and Air Quality Improvement. We had a start, but we needed more. So I put on my dancing shoes and went down to Springfield. I cajoled our state to change TIF regulations so we could apply TIFs to transportation. We also levied a first-ever fee on the ride-sharing companies Uber and Lyft, which raised $16 million in its first year (2017). We used *that* money to raise $180 million in bonds to be used for capital improvement.

We did this—the biggest modernization of our transit system in the city's history—without raising our tax rates or fare increases, and without a new federal transportation bill. Finding the money is more complicated than it should be. This is how a mayor can and must work the levers to get things done for a city.

The results from this work on the L have already been positive. The largest modernization in our mass transit's history has resulted in an increase in the rates of reliability and timeliness. Ridership for the L was up to 230 million riders a year in 2017 versus 190 million in 2007. Some 85 percent of riders report satisfaction with the service. I'm one of them; I take the L at least twice a week. When the Red Line modernization is complete, we will have twelve more trains running during rush hour. The construction will create thousands of new jobs.

I can't emphasize enough how important our mass transit systems are to our cities, and thus to our country. They are one of the biggest keys for cities to remaining competitive on the global stage. They are engines of economic growth, and they are a big part of tackling climate change and revitalizing our neighborhoods. Since the federal government has failed to take the initiative on upgrading our mass transit systems—and the rest of our infrastructure—ideas for how to fix these systems will have to come from mayors. The federal government has suggested privatizing infrastructure construction. I think that's the wrong idea. Instead we must expand existing programs that make federal-local partnerships possible. The money is already there. It just has to be utilized.

It's worth noting here that *inter*city transportation is nearly as important as city transportation. It's also an economic engine, bringing in workers from the suburbs, and it helps decongest a city and is thus good for the climate and livability. Intercity systems in our country happen to be, for the most part, younger than the subways and in less need of modernization.

If I were somehow made the infrastructure czar of the United States, here's what I would do: I would first double the funding for the Core Capacity improvement programs, which help pay for upgrades to existing corridors that are at or over capacity today or will be in five years. That would help all cities meet the challenges of rising demand. Doing this in conjunction with expanding the low-interest federal infrastructure loans would go a long way in improving our country's mass transit.

But I wouldn't stop there. The entity known as the Highway Trust Fund in the federal government mainly helps pay for roads, with just a small amount set aside for mass transit. I would shift that focus a bit, and increase the portion of the fund that supports mass transit to 25 percent. I would also raise the gas tax by twenty cents. Yes, Americans would pay more at the pump, but they would spend less time in traffic. This is a much smarter alternative to the current idea of privatizing our roads, under which we would all pay more in tolls and fees to the private investors who would own our roads and bridges. We would also pay in lost time and productivity.

This could be bigger than just transportation. I've long believed that federal transportation loans, like TIFIA and RRIF loans, could be redefined. Scale them up and move them beyond just transportation and they could become an infrastructure bank. If we could put $10 to $20 billion in the coffers there, we could spur $200 to $300 billion in projects. Cities and municipalities could take the federal equity to build projects that would become the sources for paying back the loans. This is one way the federal government could begin to heal itself.

Unfortunately, though, I don't see these reforms happening anytime soon. So solving the problem for now still falls to our cities and mayors.

———

Urban policy is, of course, also about the environment. Our cities are in fact greener than the suburbs. They waste less water on lawns. Tall buildings are more energy-efficient than rows of houses and thus reduce carbon emissions. A concentrated population also means less intrusion on natural habitats.

But by far the biggest reason that cities are green is the fact that city-dwellers drive far less than those who don't live in cities. Cars are one of the biggest environmental challenges we'll have to face as we deal with climate change, from the fossil fuels they use to the exhaust they emit. Urbanites rely less on cars, because of mass transit and density, than their suburban and rural counterparts.

My predecessor, Richard M. Daley, came up with the original Chicago Climate Action plan in 2008. I doubled down on it when I took office. My first act: shutting down the last two coal plants in the city. And then, in 2017, along with the mayors of more than fifty other cities around the world, I signed the Chicago Climate Charter. One unsung aspect of addressing climate change is retrofitting existing buildings. Through the new charter plan we signed, Chicago has begun making our commercial, industrial, and residential buildings more energy-efficient. So far the city has retrofitted 57 million square feet of building space in the city. This is good for the environment, and it saves the city's taxpayers $10.6 million a year. We enacted green standards for renovations, and we conserved water and encouraged the building of green roofs and the planting of more trees. And we started the process of replacing every streetlight in the city—some 270,000—with more energy-efficient LED lights. These lights will save the city $100 million over a decade. For all this work in energy efficiency, the EPA awarded Chicago the ENERGY STAR Partner of the Year Award. We were the only city to win the award that year.

We are well on our way not only to reaching the goals of the Paris Agreement but to exceeding them. During my tenure as mayor, our carbon emissions fell by 7 percent (as the country's emissions rose 1 percent). In that same time period, Chicago's economy *grew* 11 percent. And herein lies the "clean" little secret when it comes to tackling climate change and being an environmental steward: It's not only the right thing to do for our planet. It's also fiscally smart.

———

Another part of urban policy is, of course, the safety of the residents. Security is something the federal government plays a role in, especially when it comes to wars and terrorism. But much of the security of a city is in the hands of the city itself (even with counterterrorism), especially when it comes to nonglobal issues of safety.

You undoubtedly know about the gun violence problem we have in Chicago. The headlines make it seem worse than it actually is (we are not the most dangerous city in the country; we are twentieth on the list, which is still certainly nothing to crow about). That being said, one senseless shooting is one too many, and the hardest part of my job as mayor was visiting the parents of children who were victims of gun violence. These tragedies brought grieving parents to their knees and left communities destroyed. I made it a practice to visit these families, always away from the spotlight—in their homes, at the side of a hospital bed, or sometimes, tragically, in the funeral home. As a father of three, I knew no parent should feel alone in their darkest moments. I was always in awe and humbled by the strength and resilience they displayed in their time of deep despair. Through these dark moments, I was fortunate to form strong bonds and even friendships with these families—Cleo and Nate Pendleton and Delores Bailey, just to name a few. The Pendletons and Ms. Bailey, in addition to others, were so selfless and courageous in the way they turned personal pain into a public good; they set out to prevent other families from the same unbearable agony. I have always been tough on guns—the National Rifle Association hates me, which stems from my time in the Clinton administration, when I helped shepherd through the Federal Assault Weapons Ban and the Brady Bill. In our city, though, gun violence is something that frustrated me the most during my time as mayor.

Generally speaking, gun violence in Chicago has gotten better over the years, not worse. There's been a steady drop since the mid-1990s, when we added community police, banned assault weapons, and increased funds for after-school programs. In 2013 and 2014 we experienced the lowest homicide rate in the last fifty years. Gun violence spiked up again, tragically, in 2016, along with the rest of the country. But since then our gun violence rates have fallen steadily, by 39 percent. It's not good enough—even one murder with (or without) a gun is too many—but the progress we've made is encouraging, and we should not give up on it.

Our problem in Chicago boils down to guns falling into the wrong hands. Yes, we have segregated, impoverished neighborhoods, and we have entrenched gangs. But we wouldn't have nearly the problem we do now if gangs couldn't access guns so easily.

There was a time when Chicago had some of the strictest gun laws in the country. We had a ban on handgun ownership and a ban on gun sales. But both of those measures were struck down by federal courts, in 2010 and 2014, respectively. Our possession laws are also weak. In New York City, possession of a handgun gets a first-time offender three years in prison. In Chicago, possession results in only a year. We tried to match our possession laws with New York's, but we failed to pass the law in Springfield. Another factor: According to a Syracuse University study covering earlier years, the U.S. attorney's office in Chicago has ranked ninetieth out of ninety cities for federal gun law enforcement. This doesn't help when it comes to deterrence.

While I would like to see much stricter gun laws in our city, our reach only goes so far. According to a University of Chicago study, 60 percent of the new guns that were found to be used in gang-related shootings were bought in other states. Indiana, with its very weak state gun laws, is the biggest supplier, and is just a twenty-minute drive away.

So we didn't have a lot going for us in terms of guns. But we would never just throw our hands up and quit trying. We had to get the guns off our streets. One way we did this was to use smaller crimes as a way to get at the bigger gun issue. In 2017, 2018, and the first six months of 2019, the Chicago Police Department has set records in seizing guns and getting them off the street. As of this writing, the CPD is on course to seize a record 10,000 guns. But the supply never ends.

Another way is to try to stop the violence before it happens. We've done this with predictive policing, using data sets from the University of Chicago Crime Lab to help predict where a shooting may occur within a six-block radius. This enables us to prevent shots being fired in the first place, before the second retribution shot happens. The data inputs include statistics on cracked sidewalks, robberies, 311 and 911 calls made. When a certain threshold is met in a neighborhood, we flood the area with police. We borrowed this concept from Los Angeles, then refined it to fit Chicago.

We put strategic support centers in twelve of twenty-two districts, which run the data every eight hours to stay on top of crime trends. These centers are staffed around the clock by two cops and two data scientists from the University of Chicago. (If you are ever interested in witnessing some great cultural exchanges, sit in for a bit with two Chicago cops and two data nerds from the University of Chicago stuck in a room for eight hours at a time. Talk about cultural diversity.)

Ken Griffin, the founder and chief executive of the investment firm Citadel, pitched in $10 million in funding for our new crime measures. I raised the rest from Chicago corporations and philanthropic communities. None of the funding came from the federal government. Trump loves to talk smack about fighting crime in Chicago and other cities. But he and his government have never lifted a finger to do anything. We did. In fact, Trump only hindered our fight against gun violence. In 2017, he withheld federal criminal justice Byrne-grant funding for us because of our sanctuary-city status. Byrne-grant dollars could fund the strategic support centers in our police districts.

This use of data to fight crime (we aren't the only ones who do this—New Orleans, Los Angeles, and Louisville are among the other cities that do something similar) marks a significant difference between the old industrial city and the new digital one. It used to be that police swept streets just based on when it was one neighborhood's turn to be swept. That's no longer the case. Now cities use data so they can be predictive, taking a "smart streets" approach to law enforcement.

Speaking of law enforcement, reforming the police forces in our cities is also a significant component of fighting gun violence. Trust between community and law enforcement is essential. Those reforms have to be done in the right way. They have to be done in collaboration *with* the police and community.

It's why in the summer of 2015 we were the first city to voluntarily agree with the ACLU to monitor police activity, with a judge overseeing the agreement. Chicago in a hundred years had made seven attempts to reform its police department. Each reform effort fell short. As part of moving beyond our past, we were also the first and only city to pay reparations for civil rights violations by police, in the "Burge Victims" case, which happened in the mid-1980s. Jon Burge, former commander of the Chicago Police Department, allowed the systemic torture of two hundred African Americans to force confessions. Burge was fired and convicted of perjury. Not only did we pay reparations, we offered the victims free community college education as well. I believe this was key to the healing we needed to foster.

But as Laquan McDonald's shooting has shown, there was much more to be done to tackle an entrenched culture of abuse. It is the same culture that precipitated the violence against Freddie Gray, Michael Brown, Eric Garner, Sandra Bland, Trayvon Martin, Charles Kinsey, Philando Castile, and many others. I went in front of the full city council to address the police department's culture and tactics and acknowledge things that others only whispered about, like the "code of silence." We embarked on a set of reforms before the Justice Department finished their analysis and report. I had to listen to my own advice. Never allow a crisis to go to waste—it's the opportunity to take things you never thought possible and make them possible. The one thing the new police superintendent Eddie Johnson and I insisted on is that reform be done *with* police, not *to* the police. There was no going back on reform, but in order for it to take hold and complement our community policing approach, officers had to have a seat at the table. The superintendent and I led the initiative for change, including better training, new approaches to de-escalation, mental health, community policing, and new technology.

Before we entered the consent decree with judicial oversight, we had begun to implement nearly half the recommendations. I think the whole national debate has become unnecessarily polarized: Police union leadership reflexively oppose any and all change, from the smallest to the biggest item, while others demonize police at all costs. The debate should not be whether to reform, but what constitutes good reform and complements overall safety goals. Reform and safety cannot be achieved with a demoralized and dejected police department, and police cannot go back to the day where whatever they say goes. All too often that culture has led to abuse and abusive tactics. While this is a long road with ups and downs, I am proud of our commitment citywide, and that Chicago during this process never had the violence and civil disobedience associated with Ferguson, Baltimore, Milwaukee, or Charlotte during their reforms. We had a big, loud, and vigorous debate but it was free of violence, and I believe that has helped us begin the necessary journey of reform, and also helped us see significant reductions in violent crime since 2016.

Closing off access to guns, the use of predictive policing, and working with the police and community for reform all had an immediate effect on Chicago. In 2017 we had 166 fewer homicides than the year before. In 2018 we had 97 fewer on top of that. In Englewood, a South Side neighborhood that had one of our worst gun violence problems, shootings dropped to their lowest rate in the last two decades in 2017. In 2018 the drop in shootings broke another twenty-year record. Our robberies, burglaries, and auto thefts are at a twenty-one-year low. Our gun seizures are at a twenty-year high. This data indicates that we can and should make all these efforts to stem gun violence. But the only way to make lasting progress will be if we provide our young men with alternatives to guns and gangs. As I said in my second inaugural address, when young men join gangs in search of praise, we can and must do better. When young men turn to lives of crime for hope, we can and must do better. When prison is the place where we send boys to become men, we can and must do better.

I believe our reforms in education will help continue this trend. So will the modernization of the L and our neighborhood- and community-building efforts. And another program that flies under the radar has also had a huge impact.

Prevention is a huge part of this, maybe the biggest. What we want to do, ideally, is stop the formation of another lost generation, to destroy the allure of gangs, financially, culturally, and in a familial sense. Adding 1,000 police to the streets helps with this. So does our summer jobs program, which enrolls 33,000 kids now in a broad range of jobs, from cleaning to coding (there are some 65,000 applicants for this program; this is an area where we could really use some federal resources).

But the most rewarding prevention method for me is our mentoring program. Back in 2001, an organization affiliated with the University of Chicago called Youth Guidance started a school program called Becoming a Man (BAM). It requires students to meet every day for a number of hours with a trauma-trained counselor, who talks to them about the challenges in their lives. The students learn relaxation and meditation techniques, and they try out new activities together, like martial arts and archery. The idea is to help the students cope with such feelings as frustration and to "think about their thinking." This is vitally important: Much of the violence we see in our cities is impulsive, an overreaction to provocation.

I loved the program from the beginning, and I did much to enhance and boost its reach. We funded some of it from a $10.4 million settlement we received after we sued Uber and Lyft for inadequate background checks on their drivers. This idea was hatched at the University of Chicago Crime Lab. We started to scale it up, and it now reaches 7,000 young men and is being copied by other cities, such as Boston. The goal is to reach all young men in crime-ridden neighborhoods by ensuring they are in a mentoring program from seventh to eleventh grades. Chicago is on track to achieve that goal this year. Now that I have left City Hall, I have agreed to be national chair to expand BAM's reach beyond Chicago.

This, to me, is such a great example of what's going on in cities these days. As the federal government has receded as an investor and facilitator to local progress (in all areas, not just crime prevention and mentoring), universities, nonprofits, and local public sectors have come together to find the resources and the intellectual and financial willpower to make things happen. In Chicago, there is an impactful mentoring program (which I will delve into) that was hatched by a university, and then moved along by the city with some swiftness, without any help from the federal government. This sort of thing also happened with Bloomberg's tech center, which was a partnership among industry, universities, and the local government, and in the 2014 bailout of Detroit, which was worked out by the state of Michigan and various philanthropies, such as the Ford Foundation. This coming together of entities within a city to solve a problem, create a new program, or innovate is another paradigm shift that we are going through. In the spaces where the federal government once took the lead, cities and all of the entities within them are filling the void.

I've taken part in BAM sessions. In 2012, I asked President Obama to come to one during a visit to Chicago. Initially he demurred, citing a busy schedule. I begged. "I quit my job and moved my family to D.C. to work for you," I told him. "Just twenty minutes." After some more begging, he finally said yes. That twenty minutes turned into an hour and a half and if you know President Obama, who is meticulously on time, that is a big deal. President Obama was blown away, and that experience formed the basis of his nationwide mentoring program, My Brother's Keeper. (The young man he sat next to during his BAM session, Christian, introduced the president when the president launched My Brother's Keeper at the White House. Christian is now on his way to graduate from Western Illinois University.)

I also encouraged Bill Gates, whose wife, Melinda, said the program "changed him," and the Cubs general manager, Theo Epstein, to attend sessions. (I'm leaning hard on the NBA to make BAM its top funding priority when it comes to their non-profit outreach. The players and coaches would be a perfect fit for the program.) The Reinsdorf family and the entire Bulls team have stepped in in a big way, and I can't thank them enough.

BAM has made a huge difference in the lives of our school-children. In 2018, I received a letter from a senior at Marshall High School on the West Side, who wrote that he "never saw or met any males like me who led successful lives" until he entered the BAM program, which turned his life around (he referred to his mentor as "Pops"). He enrolled at Mississippi Valley State University in the fall of 2018. But the results of the program are not just anecdotal. A University of Chicago study showed that BAM cut youth violent crime arrests in Chicago by 50 percent, and raised the high school graduation rates of its participants by 20 percent. We cannot keep sending our boys to prison and hope—and expect—that they will become men. This program has begun to help rescue an entire generation that otherwise would have been forgotten and left to the streets for their education and development. This is a letter I read to the full city council during my final budget hearing to expand BAM to seventh-grade boys:

Dear Mr. Mayor.

My name is Rajay Montgomery. I am a senior at John Marshall High School, located on the west side of Chicago. I would like to begin my journey before becoming a life-member of BAM. I'm a good kid, a good person, but I was experiencing some rough patches and had some negative notions. I felt that no one really cared about me except my mother and grandma.

Was I a concerned or productive student? Nah, that wasn't me. I couldn't focus, I often asked myself, why am I here? Why come to school?

Freshman year, I never saw or met any males that looked like me lead successful lives. Day after day, I saw men on the streets using or selling drugs. These were people I personally knew, and I was growing up around them. I saw them give up on school because of lack of support.

My sophomore year, second semester, I joined BAM. Since joining, I noticed that my street habits left. I've become more invested in my life and involved in school. My attendance is better, my mental focus is better, and all this has showed up in my grades. They are amazing.

I observed my BAM peers at school gain confidence in themselves and because of that, a lot of good things started happening for them.

Mr. Dorsey, also known as "My Pops," was the BAM counselor at Marshall. He recruited me. He helped me out every single day, not just during school hours, but whenever I needed him. My pops is always there. He challenged me daily, drilled integrity, accountability, self-determination, positive anger expression, respect for womanhood, and visionary goal setting. Our BAM core values.

He always made us feel like we belonged, and we were important.

After I graduate high school in June 2019, I plan to attend Mississippi Valley State University. I plan to major in business. And of course, Mr. Dorsey helped me get in the University. He took me there on a college tour.

Because of him and BAM, I will continue to chase my

dreams and focus on myself and make sure that I become very successful in life because I must pay it forward. Mr. Mayor, I'm just saying thank you for supporting Youth Guidance and BAM. Meeting Mr. Dorsey changed my life. Thank you to you and the people of the City of Chicago for supporting us.

Best,

Rajay Montgomery

We are not yet where we want to be when it comes to gun violence in Chicago. Not even close. But the steps we've taken have made progress and given us hope. Rajay, Christian, and the other young men like them are leading the way.

I want to talk about one more thing we've done in Chicago that involves the safety of our citizens. I touched on it earlier when talking about Nan Whaley and Dayton, Ohio: the opioid crisis that we're in the midst of in this country.

The epidemic has killed more Americans than the wars in Vietnam and Iraq combined. In 2017 alone, about 50,000 Americans died of an opioid overdose, around 130 people a day. The annual cost of the epidemic to the country is $79 billion. And those statistics don't take into account all the wreckage inflicted by opioid addiction and abuse—the families torn apart, the jobs and careers lost, the health-care costs, all of that human potential spoiled.

The federal government has taken some steps of late in addressing the crisis, and I applaud it for that. But in most cases that effort has fallen short and come a bit late. The Federal Drug Administration was slow to regulate the drugs. It doesn't help that some big pharmaceutical companies have their moneyed hooks deep into that organization. The only public fight I ever had with the Obama administration was over opioids. The Department of Health and Human Services ruled that opioids could be prescribed to adolescents. I met then-HHS head Sylvia Matthews Burwell in her office and pleaded with her to reverse that ruling. "Sylvia," I said, "this is a full-blown crisis. And you should know that." Burwell was from West Virginia, the epicenter of the crisis. We argued for a while to no avail.

Sometime in 2014 a friend of mine handed me an advance copy of a forthcoming book. "You have to read this" is all he said. The book was called *Dreamland: The True Tale of America's Opiate Epidemic*, and it was written by a journalist named Sam Quinones. It told the tale of how the epidemic began and then boomed, and how pushes by Big Pharma and Mexican drug dealers worked in concert to create addicts and destroy entire communities across the country. I read the book in one weekend.

I had some background with pharmaceutical companies. In my first term in the U.S. House of Representatives, I took them on for the price-gouging they had been imposing on American consumers. My pharmaceutical reimportation bill, which I worked on with a Republican colleague, Gil Gutknecht from Minnesota, was my first big win as a congressman in the House. It gave American consumers the right to buy cheaper drugs from other countries, but, no surprise, Big Pharma killed the legislation in the Senate.

I'd also watched many of the Big Tobacco hearings on the Hill and had read the documents that uncovered their plot to conceal the truth about their products from the American people. So, once again, I knew enough to be dangerous.

Dreamland shook me. The parallels between Big Pharma and Big Tobacco were chilling. The pharmaceutical executives knew that their products were killing people, and yet they were doing nothing to stop it. Quite the opposite, in fact. They were pushing their products like street dealers.

Chicago is not unlike a lot of places in the country. It has been hit hard by the epidemic. Opioid-related visits to Chicago hospitals increased 65 percent from 2004 to 2011. Emergency rooms in the city were fielding more than 1,000 visits each year due to the abuse or misuse of opioids. The epidemic wasn't confined just to the city. Suburban kids were driving into Chicago to buy opiates on what was known as the "Heroin Highway." News coverage frequently showed disturbing scenes of teens who had overdosed at gas stations on their way back out of the city.

I got my team together, and we studied our options. We held a conference with surrounding counties, since the crisis knew no borders. And we formulated a plan.

In the summer of 2014, I announced that the city of Chicago was suing five of the nation's largest opioid manufacturers— Purdue Pharma, Cephalon, Janssen Pharmaceuticals, Endo Health Solutions, and Activis—because for years they had actively deceived the public about the true risks of highly potent and highly addictive painkillers. They just wanted to make more money. Enough was enough.

Soon afterward other cities filed their own lawsuits, and it's true that imitation is the sincerest form of flattery. After Mayor Whaley and Dayton filed theirs, it all snowballed. Hundreds of other cities all across the country have since joined in what's become a widespread class-action lawsuit.

There were some who questioned our decision. After all, our

suburbs are home to some big pharmaceutical companies, like Abbott Laboratories, and these companies provided many jobs. But the crisis overrode any of these concerns.

We didn't just stop there. In 2018 we sued the three biggest opioid distributors—AmerisourceBergen, Cardinal Health, and McKesson—for unlawful and unfettered distribution in the city and for endangering public health. We also passed a law that requires every pharmacy in the city to provide the names of the five doctors who prescribe opioids most often so we can better monitor them. We held a joint conference with our suburban counties to coordinate both public health and public safety efforts on this issue.

But it wasn't enough to just nab the dealers: We had to help prevent addiction, and help those who had succumbed to it as well. In 2018 we passed an ordinance that limited opioid prescriptions to city employees to seven days, unless the illness or surgery was life-threatening. We passed another one in 2016 that created a license requirement for pharmaceutical representatives. In order to practice, these representatives had to pay a $750 fee. That money went into a fund for opioid treatment and rehabilitation. So far that money has helped nearly 3,000 people and counting.

———

A few decades ago, our federal government would have been the primary actor in nearly everything I talk about above. They would have spearheaded the mass transit funding, the help needed for disadvantaged city neighborhoods, the protection of the environment, the task of confronting gun violence, mentoring youth, and the opioid epidemic.

That's no longer the case. These problems, in some combination or another, exist in all of our cities. The solutions—and the hope—reside there, too.

I told you earlier about the three sets of lists I kept while I was mayor—one with the daily tasks, one with the weekly ones, and one with my biggest goals. As my tenure as mayor came down to its last few months, I spent a lot of time looking at that last list. There were some big goals that I was unable to reach. I couldn't completely rid my city of guns. I couldn't lift every man, woman, and child out of poverty. But I am proud of the progress the city made while I had the privilege of running it. I remember some of the goals that used to be on that list—the O'Hare expansion, the Riverwalk, universal full-day pre-K, free community college, the minimum-wage increase, the tech campus—and think about how gratifying it was to cross them off. More important than checking them off the list is their impact on the residents of the city who are better prepared to make the most of their future. In the end, that's the yardstick we measure ourselves by. I think we've learned as a city how resourceful and resilient we can be, and that makes me believe that our future is brighter— with Mayor Lori Lightfoot and all the mayors to come—than it's ever been.

What you see happening is a new paradigm emerging at the local level. It is replacing the federal-local partnership that existed in the past with universities, nonprofits, philanthropists, and the local public sector. The Chicago Star Scholarship, BAM, neighborhood revitalization—these are all reflections and manifestations of the new paradigm and the new model that are emerging at local levels and replacing the role of the federal government because of the void that's been created.

NINE

International Mayors

Whenever I talk to Bruce Katz, the former Brookings Institution scholar and a leading thinker when it comes to the growing power, influence, and potential of cities, he always mentions one word to me: Copenhagen.

The reason: Copenhagen is an exemplar of the modern city. Its economy is robust and diversified, as it is a center of finance, science, and shipping. It has some of the highest employee wages in the world. The city is super-aggressive when it comes to dealing with climate change and is well on its way to meeting its goal of becoming carbon-neutral by 2025. Most of its residents use bicycles as their primary mode of transportation, and the city has a mandate that there must be either a park or a beach within a fifteen-minute walk of every city resident. Copenhagen has twenty-two Michelin-rated restaurants. And it's ranked as one of the happiest cities in the world by the United Nations. Copenhagen comes very close to hitting the uber-city trifecta: It's a great place to live, work, and play.

It wasn't always like that, though. As I mentioned earlier, it wasn't too long ago that Copenhagen was in crisis, verging on bankruptcy and suffering through close to 18 percent unemployment. Right around that time, in 1989, the people of Copenhagen elected a former math and Danish teacher named Jens Kramer Mikkelsen as their new mayor.

To face the daunting task of revitalizing his city, Mikkelsen decided to embark on major infrastructure projects, which would improve the city's quality of life and attract businesses and more residents. The problem was that he had no clear way of financing his plan. The Danish national government wasn't going to pay for it, and he couldn't raise taxes on a populace that was already under economic stress. So he came up with the idea of taking a huge swath of underutilized land owned by the city, some of it around the harbor and some of it in the downtown area, and transferring it to a publicly owned but privately led company, which would eventually be called the Copenhagen City & Port Development Corporation. (Mikkelsen took over the company after he left his mayoral post in 2004.) The land was rezoned for residential and commercial use and for parks. The city used the projected revenues generated by the new infrastructure to build a mass transit system that connected the redeveloped areas to the rest of the city. The new construction—the buildings and the parks—was done in an environmentally friendly way, in accordance with the city's climate goals.

The result is that thirty years after the city's nadir, Copenhagen has, as Katz has written, "a vibrant, multipurpose waterfront. A world-class transit system. Thousands of housing units built for market and social purposes." Mikkelsen's initiative, he writes, was "nothing short of transformative."

Katz believes that what Copenhagen did will ultimately flow throughout the world. "It really is a model for how mayors should govern and how cities can lead our world today," he says.

———

When it comes to cities and their mayors, national borders mean less and less. Our global world is connected through its cities. People, capital, ideas, innovation, and culture all flow from city to city with little regard for national borders. "Our mayors and cities have a local approach with a global principle," says former Montreal mayor Denis Coderre. "Everybody is related to everybody. We live, learn, and survive together."

Ideas and innovations are being turned into practical applications in cities around the world. Stuttgart (with its Morgenstadt), Seoul (with its Sharing City), and Barcelona (with its Urban Lab) are just a few of the world's cities that have created and emphasized innovation labs as a critical part of their present and future economy. And speaking of Barcelona, that city has moved ahead—without any help from the Spanish national government—to make its mass transit systems digital, which will help the system become more reliable, efficient, and responsive to consumer expectations. Large-scale bike-sharing programs, which reduce congestion and pollution, were first started in Copenhagen. Vancouver, which already has the smallest carbon footprint of any major city in North America, has embarked on an ambitious initiative (called Greenest City 2020 Action Plan) to completely eliminate its dependence on fossil fuels, walking the walk as its home country continues to merely talk the talk. Tel Aviv has become a leader in green technology. And Lyon, France, has created a publicly owned, privately run company to rejuvenate land in its inner city and on the Rhône River. Katz was right—other cities did follow Copenhagen's lead.

The dynamism of cities isn't just relegated to what we think of as "developed countries." Taipei, located in emerging Taiwan, is a leader in industrial design. The São Pedro neighborhood of Belo Horizonte in Brazil is home to more than three hundred start-ups. Ho Chi Minh City in Vietnam is emerging as a leader in Asia in blockchain start-ups. India's Bangalore, once a manufacturing city, is now a software hub and city of ideas. And the investments that Gaborone has made in education—at all levels—have paid off and helped it become a beacon of hope and progress in Botswana.

This dynamism and progress matters, not only for the cities but for everyone in the world. Cities are our pathway to the future, and because of the growing interconnectedness of our cities, our world will rise as they do.

———

On May 5, 2016, Sadiq Khan was elected the mayor of London, gaining more votes than any politician in Great Britain's history. The son of Pakistani immigrants, Khan is a practicing Muslim (he fasts for a month each year for Ramadan) and in his own way is a living metaphor for the mayors of today, who are at once global and local. (England has had directly elected mayors since 2000.)

Khan's progressive efforts in the areas of transit, climate change, and inclusiveness have set London on a positive path for the future. He faced an enormous challenge just a month and a half into his tenure as mayor, when his country voted to exit the European Union. Khan has not backed down in the face of

Brexit and its potentially catastrophic effects on his city and has instead fought hard to retain London's preeminent place in the world.

Income equality is a major issue for London, just as it is for every one of the world's great cities. Khan realized early on that accessible and affordable mass transit is one significant way to address the issue, by giving lower-income citizens of his city the literal and figurative transportation to a better life. One of his first actions as mayor was to freeze fares on much of his city's mass transit. The freeze, which includes fares on buses, trams, "pay as you go" Tube rides, and bike shares, benefits around 4 million journeys a day. Khan also introduced the unlimited Hopper fare, which allows people to change buses as many times as they want while paying only once within an hour. Again, this helped lower-income residents the most, since they rely more heavily on bus transport than other residents and sometimes have longer commutes into the city that require more than one bus ride. "We are putting money back into people's pockets," says Khan. He has also spearheaded the effort to increase usage of mass transit, getting what's known as the Night Tube and the Overground Night Service up and running, thus giving Londoners twenty-four-hour train service on Fridays and Saturdays, which were traditionally dead periods for mass transit.

Of course, more affordable mass transit means more riders and less congestion and pollution. In concert with that, Khan has invested millions of dollars in bicycling and walking infrastructure in the city. London, like most cities, has too many cars. Khan wanted to address that issue now and get ahead of it for the future. London's population is expected to increase from 8.8 million now to 9.8 million by 2030. Khan doesn't want the population explosion to mean an explosion in cars. "Our goal is

to increase the proportion of people walking, cycling, and taking public transport to 80 percent of their journeys by 2041," he says.

These transit efforts cost money, of course. Khan has not had a bit of help from his national government. In fact, it's been a hindrance, if anything. What was once an annual $800 million national grant for London's transportation has been phased out. The city is on its own.

London is also in need of expanded airport capacity. The national government voted for a plan to add a runway to Heathrow Airport, a decision made hastily after two decades of debate. Though London, like Chicago and Los Angeles, needs the capacity, Khan says the Heathrow expansion "is just the wrong decision." His reason: the harmful effects a new Heathrow runway would have on air quality, noise pollution, and public transport in the city. The Heathrow expansion has been tied up in the courts and likely will be for some time.

Instead Khan has backed a more innovative, and saner, proposal to add a runway to Gatwick Airport instead. "The expansion could be delivered more quickly and cheaply and with fewer negative impacts," he says. (Gatwick is in a less densely populated area outside the city.) Gatwick already has the land available, and the airport has kept it open in case Khan—and common sense—prevail.

To Khan, tackling climate change is also a commonsense issue. Under him, London has taken some aggressive steps. Though Great Britain has stayed in the Paris Agreement (unlike the United States), Khan believes his country's efforts and plans on climate change still fall short. So London will lead the way. It is the first megacity in the world to make the pledge to become carbon-neutral by 2050, and it's already taken some significant steps toward reaching that goal. (Khan is also divesting the city's pension funds of fossil fuel investments.) While London was once a laggard when it came to solar power, the city now outperforms the country in terms of new solar panel deployment. Low-emission transportation and improved energy efficiency guidelines for homes and businesses in London are also more ambitious than those of the national government.

Khan has enlisted the private sector to help with the environment. He's brought together the city's eleven largest employers, which include Tesco, Sky, and Siemens, in a program that will cut levels of pollution and emissions that far exceed targets set by Parliament. The companies have pledged to use 100 percent renewable energy in their buildings by 2020 and to transition to a zero-emission vehicle fleet by 2025. "This is not just an environmental issue," says Khan. "It's a health issue as well." Studies have shown that about 9,500 Londoners die every year because of their exposure to the polluted air. Khan also implemented a toxicity charge for the most polluting vehicles in the city, and in 2019 he opened the world's first ultra-low-emissions zone, targeting London's badly polluted central district. Vehicles traveling in the zone must either meet tighter new emissions standards or pay a fine. This is an idea that other cities have tried but failed to implement. I'm hoping London shows us the way.

———

Like many European capitals, London has had to confront issues of immigration and changing demographics, with all of the promise and peril that they bring. The tragic Grenfell Tower fire in 2017 was in many ways a microcosm of this issue. The tower housed many new immigrants, who play a vital role in London's global economy. The building was constructed hastily and with shoddy materials, and many of those immigrants paid the ulti-

mate price for that negligence. Cities all over the world face similar issues with huge numbers of newly arrived immigrants. How
do we take care of them? How do we ensure that they are safe
and given an opportunity to succeed? There is no easy answer.
But one thing is for sure: Turning them away is not the right
answer. London, like most great cities in the world, has declared
itself a welcoming city, and it is already one of the most diverse
places in the world, with more than three hundred different lan-
guages spoken every day. "We celebrate, cherish, and embrace
diversity," Khan says. "And we continue to do all we can to show
that we are open to everyone, regardless of race, age, religion,
disability, or sexuality."

Khan appointed the city's first-ever deputy mayor for social
integration, social mobility, and community engagement to
spearhead an effort to forge stronger relationships among London's diverse communities. He's also had his government lead by
example when it comes to hiring practices. Within City Hall, he
published the first-ever gender and ethnicity pay audit, and he
has used his bully pulpit to encourage all London businesses—
and the national government—to do the same.

The thorniest issue Khan has faced is, of course, Brexit and
all the fallout and uncertainty that ensued from that decision.
In June 2016, when the citizens of the United Kingdom voted
to leave the European Union, they effectively turned their backs
on the world (this may sound familiar to citizens of the U.S.,
who did a similar thing just five months later). Khan immediately began to fight to keep London facing forward. He had to:
His city's future is at stake. "I'm determined to keep banging
the drum for London, getting the message out loud and clear
around the world that despite Brexit, London remains open to
the world," he says. "Open to business, open to ideas, open to

investment, open to trade, and open to talent." (Greater London was the only area in England that voted to stay with the EU.)

Khan has traveled all over the world, including to Chicago, to spread the word and promote his city. He knows that the survival of London as one of the preeminent cities in the world—and, to be sure, the survival of his country (London is responsible for 30 percent of his country's tax revenues)—requires him to go on the offensive. He has done what he can to chart an independent economic and cultural strategy around Brexit, forging alliances with other cities (including Chicago).

Yes, all of this will be extremely difficult. Khan is up against it, for sure. But he knows he cannot stand still. Even with the headwinds, he has no other choice but to try to create a degree of separation between his city and his national government.

———

The mayor of Milan, Giuseppe Sala, has a clear-eyed view of his country's national government. Put simply, it's chaotic. In the last seventy-five years, Italy has had more than sixty national governments. Stability in the country comes from the mayors and its great cities, like Sala and Milan.

That stability has allowed Milan to prosper. The city's population has increased by 8 percent since 2012, spurred on by more young residents. Sala, who became mayor in 2016, has been active in recruiting newcomers and making them more likely to stay, using his experience in the private sector—he was formerly in management at Pirelli, among other companies—to get the city to work for itself.

Sala says that globalism is here to stay and that immigrants comprise the entrepreneurial workforce that makes cities go. He has declared Milan an open city, which he describes as a "very sensitive battle" with his national government. "My fellow citizens have asked that we remain open, open to the world and to investment and growth. We feel the pressure from those on the outside who do not want this, but the reality is that this is the future of our city and the world."

At the heart of Sala's big plans for Milan is making it a better place to live and work. He has focused on boosting the role of the universities in the city to help fire up the city's economic engine. Some of the universities have begun construction on inner-city campuses. (Having such campuses is a norm in the United States but a new thing for Italy.) The result is a university student population that has grown from 130,000 to 200,000 in just the last few years. The curricula in the universities reflects a global approach: Most of them now are offering classes taught in English for the first time.

Sala has also set forth an infrastructure plan that includes hundreds of acres of green space, the addition of a fifth subway line, and 1.5 million square feet of refurbished rail lines. The green spaces will beautify the city and make it more livable, and the mass transit upgrades will make the city easier to traverse. The latter, too, goes hand in hand with his goal of reducing the number of private cars in the city. In 1993, Milan had seventy-three cars per one hundred citizens. Sala says that number has now been reduced to fifty, and his goal is to get it down to forty by 2030. He's also instituted prohibitions and fees on vehicles in the downtown area of the city and has narrowed, as opposed to broadened, the major thoroughfares, which slows down traffic. A brighter future with fewer cars—and less pollution and congestion—is his vision, pushing his city on a faster path than that of his national government. "It is costly and it all takes time," he says. "But at the end of the day, it is our only option."

The fifth subway line is a part of this plan, too. The new line, which is scheduled to open in 2022, will provide a public transport option to the airport. The ride from downtown, Sala says, will take just fourteen minutes and will cost all of $2.

Milan, of course, is also known for its excellent food. Sala is making it known for its excellent food policies. In 2018 he instituted a food distribution plan that connects the city's restaurants with its public schools and lower-income residents. Many cities have Meals on Wheels–type programs, but Milan's far exceeds those programs. Some 700 million tons of food were donated in the program's first six months, including 80,000 meals that went to schools. Sala incentivized the local food establishments to take part in the program by offering a tax break. "Food is part of our heritage and now we are using that heritage in a new way," he says. "This is the type of innovation, the blending of the old and the new, that we can do in our cities."

———

"In a globalized world, protectionist reflexes can only separate us and spread fear," says Anne Hidalgo, the decidedly outward-facing mayor of Paris. Under her leadership, the birthplace of the Age of Enlightenment has remained true to its heritage, with innovative ideas and programs involving immigration, climate change, and the new economy.

Hidalgo became the city's first female mayor after serving for thirteen years as the deputy mayor. She's had her work cut out for her. Like many major cities in Europe, Paris has been on the front line of the flow of refugees, men and women and children fleeing war, persecution, and poverty who have put their lives at risk and who have sometimes lost everything in order to stay alive and try to find a better life for themselves.

While national governments have been slow to respond to this issue—if they've responded at all—or, in some cases, have opted for a protectionist stance, Hidalgo has decided that Paris will be proactive and welcoming. Her own experience has perhaps played a role in this. Hidalgo is the daughter of Spanish immigrants—an electrician and a seamstress—who left Spain during the reign of Francisco Franco, the Spanish dictator who was fond of forced labor and concentration camps and executions. Her story isn't too different from those of the current refugees.

In 2015, Hidalgo mobilized the Parisian community around two pillars to shelter the refugees: She's further developed the existing food and health monitoring processes to respond to the basic human needs of the refugees and any emergencies, and she's developed a structure to help ease the reception of the refugees as they arrive by, for instance, teaching them the French language, which is a key to successful integration. She opened two centers—one for male refugees and one for female refugees—"so we can receive those seeking refuge with some dignity," she says.

The French national government, though, shut down these centers and returned to a policy of undocumented refugee camps in 2018. "This did not meet all of their needs," says Hidalgo. So she defied the national government. Thousands of Parisians, at her urging, have continued to teach French classes, serve food, and provide refugees with places to stay, and she has also established a bill of rights for the refugees in her city. In 2019 she reopened the refugee centers that the French government had closed. This is the way forward, she believes, even in the face of ISIS-related attacks in Paris. "We know that this phenomenon of migration is here to stay, and we all need to address it together," she says. "A lack of reflection and coordination at the national and European levels has translated into inward-looking attitudes and national populisms. It is necessary to be building for the long term and at a European scale. And integration has to be our goal. There are no other sustainable solutions."

Hidalgo has also taken her fight to *our* national government when it comes to the issue of climate change. "Mr. Trump does not decide who opts into the Paris Agreement," she said when Trump pulled the United States out of the international agreement. "Cities do." Hidalgo has upheld, and at times surpassed, the agreement that bears her city's name. In 2016 she launched something known as Paris Breathes (Paris Respire), which closed certain roads to car traffic on Sundays between the hours of 9 a.m. and 5 p.m. She has set the city up to ban all diesel-powered vehicles by 2025 (this is no easy feat; many vehicles in Europe still run on air-fouling diesel engines). Both sides of the Seine are now prohibited to car traffic and have become beautiful pedestrian areas (more on this in a bit). She has championed urban agriculture and opened many new gardens and parks in the city. And by 2015, there were 435 miles of bicycle lanes in Paris.

Her overarching strategic plan is bold: to achieve carbon neutrality and a city fully converted to renewable energies by 2050. "These actions are both urgent and practical," she says.

Hidalgo believes that climate health goes hand in hand with a healthy economy. Paris has in recent decades been a business and financial economy. Hidalgo has worked to diversify the economy and bring in more of a tech focus. Paris has become a city of incubators and start-ups. The city now has eighty incubators, which work directly with Parisian universities. Hidalgo says there are some 6,000 university students who are hosted by them each year, which helps foster future careers. These incubators and university graduates have helped create 10,000 new start-up companies in Paris, creating countless new jobs. "This has created a bubbling and generous ecosystem," says Hidalgo. "This is what cities are uniquely able to do."

———

European mayors aren't the only ones getting things done on the international stage. In 2018, Souad Abderrahim became the first female and Islamist mayor of the Arab city of Tunis, Tunisia. That feat alone is enough of an accomplishment, but the fact that Abderrahim has focused her first few years in office on rebuilding the city's infrastructure and the environment places her right alongside the most progressive mayors in the world. Beng Climaco, the mayor of Zamboanga City in the Philippines, survived a siege early on in her tenure to emerge as a fierce advocate of the environment and food security, two long-standing problems in her city. Clover Moore, the mayor of Sydney, Australia, has ushered her already environmentally friendly city to even new heights, converting the city fleet to hybrid vehicles, building the largest solar photovoltaic system in the city's history, and harvesting water in city parks. Moore has also overseen an infrastructure boom in Sydney, which has resulted in eight major new buildings, with more in the pipeline.

I've written about these international mayors because of the interconnectedness of cities in our global world. Goods and services no longer see national borders. Ideas don't, either. We're in an age when many citizens feel frustrated with national governments. For many in these nations, the response has been to hunker down into nativism and angry populism. That, to me, is not the answer to our global problems and never has been. Instead, as these mayors demonstrate, the path to a stronger, healthier world is through a more tolerant progressivism. This is the way the world should be going, and it's the way to solve our problems and get things done. And it is our mayors, both internationally and nationally, who are showing us the way.

TEN

Cities, Waterfronts, and Riverwalks

Chicago is a city of water. Lake Michigan, with its clarity and sandy beaches, is our front yard. The lakefront was treasured by Chicago's forefathers, from DuSable to Montgomery Ward. They decided more than a century ago that it should be forever protected and open and never be industrialized or privatized. As a result, twenty-five of our twenty-nine lakefront miles are public parkland. (Chicago was the only major Great Lakes city to do this.) That wise decision by the city's forefathers has had a long-lasting effect: It has undeniably made Chicago a better place to live—healthier, more aesthetically pleasing, less congested, and more environmentally friendly. The beaches are an urban oasis.

Then there was our great "dark river," as Nelson Algren once described it, our forgotten waterway or, as I like to say, Lake Michigan's younger sibling. The Chicago River is short in distance but long in importance, perhaps the single biggest factor in the rise of the city. Flowing through the city's heart, it connects Chicago to Lake Michigan, the Great Plains, the Mississippi River, the Gulf of Mexico, and ultimately the rest of the world. The industries that sprang up on its banks in the nineteenth and early twentieth centuries—tanning factories, lumber and steel mills, stockyards—helped transform Chicago from a rather sleepy town of 30,000 inhabitants in 1850 to a vibrant commercial hub of the country with a population of 1.5 million just fifty years later.

Unlike Lake Michigan, the Chicago River was viewed only as a commercial thruway, subservient to the industries it accommodated. This viewpoint led to some serious negative effects. By the late nineteenth century the river was severely polluted, filled with the effluent of its shoreline factories, from toxic metals to slaughterhouse offal. A portion of the South Branch of the river was once known as Bubbly Creek because of the carbonic gases that rose to the surface from decomposing entrails dumped into it by the slaughterhouses. The pollution got so bad that the city reversed the flow of the river away from Lake Michigan in 1900 because it was fouling the supply of drinking water. There was never any real public access to the river. No one would have wanted to be too close to it anyway.

Some of the city's forefathers, though, did see a different future for the Chicago River. Foremost among them was Daniel Burnham, the master architect of the city and the man who was in charge of the 1893 World's Columbian Exposition in Chicago, at the time the largest expo in history. In 1909, in one of his master plans for the city, Burnham suggested rethinking the river's shorelines, opening them up and lining them with a vast promenade. Burnham's original vision was of Chicago as a two-waterfront city. It was never acted upon. More than eight decades later, Burnham's idea was revived. In the early 2000s, preparations were made for a riverside park, and a few areas were cleared for construction. But then the project halted, stunted by a lack of funding. What a shock, what a surprise. The idea was left for dead.

Both the Crawford and Fisk coal plants were located on the South Branch of the Chicago River. After we shut them down, the era of the river being used solely as an industrial highway was officially—and finally—over. We built four boathouses in different neighborhoods, so recreation on the river had begun to take off. It is now growing exponentially. The question then became, what more can we now do to bring the river back to life. That was followed by another question: How could we possibly pay for whatever we want to do?

———

In October 2011, just a few months into my tenure as mayor of Chicago, I traveled to Little Rock, Arkansas, to attend a reunion of former Bill Clinton staffers. We went to celebrate the twentieth anniversary of the day that Clinton announced his candidacy for president of the United States.

At this point City Hall was up and running and I had all but one of my staff positions filled. That last one, though, was an important one. I had laid out an ambitious agenda for Chicago already, and had plans—on that list in my drawer—for even bigger and bolder things. I needed money to fund those plans. I wasn't going to find it in Chicago alone—I was busy chipping away at the city's $635 million operating deficit. I wasn't going to get any more money than I was already receiving from the state. In fact, it was more likely that we would be getting *less*: The state of Illinois had $47 billion in debt when I became mayor. I knew the federal government wasn't suddenly going to enact new laws and start directing projects and handing out money to us for infrastructure, schooling, and housing. I did know, however, that the federal government actually *had* money that wasn't being utilized, and that we could again try to find and utilize it. I just needed someone to help me, someone on my staff who was smart, aggressive, and well versed in the way Washington, D.C., worked.

I knew exactly the right person for that job. And I knew I'd see her at the Clinton reunion.

When Melissa Green was nineteen, she worked in the war room for the Clinton campaign, reporting to James Carville. After Clinton's election she got a job working for Gene Sperling at the National Economic Council. Later, during the Obama administration, Green worked for Pete Orszag at the Office of Management and Budget. I knew her well from all of these stops. She was whip-smart. I nicknamed her "the Missile," because when she discovered where the money was hidden, she was like a heat-seeking missile going after it. She had left the Obama administration to work in the private sector right around the time I had left to run for mayor.

I spotted Green at the party on the first night of the Clinton reunion. I walked up to her and tapped her on the shoulder. Before she could say anything, I asked her, "Are you coming to work for me? I want an answer by the end of the night."

Thankfully, she said yes.

I took some grief back home for the hire, because Green had no connection at all to Chicago. But I didn't care. She knew D.C. like the back of her hand. She would have her work cut out for her. There was no such thing as "easy money" anymore. Earmarks, that funding that congressmen had for years been slipping into spending bills to pay for pet projects back in their home districts, had been banned. But if anyone knew where the money was buried and how to access it, it was Green. Her work at the OMB and the relationships she had built over the years would certainly come in handy.

After I hired Green, I started traveling to D.C. once every six weeks or so. She and I would meet with different members of Obama's cabinet and probe for funds. One of those members was the secretary of transportation, a man named Ray LaHood.

I'd known LaHood for a while, and we were the best of friends. He was a former Republican U.S. congressman from Illinois, serving the Peoria area. When I served in Congress, he and I often flew back to Chicago from D.C. together. Whenever I had a seat ahead of him on the plane, I would switch with him just before we landed, so he'd have a better chance of making his connecting flight to Peoria. We frequently cohosted off-the-record, casual steak dinners in D.C. for a bipartisan group of legislators from across the country. President Obama had chosen him for his cabinet position at my strong suggestion. I would like everybody to think about this for a moment: Ray is the son of a Lebanese immigrant, I am the son of an Israeli immigrant. Ray is a Republican, I am a Democrat. Ray is from downstate, and I'm from Chicago. If we can find common ground and build a lifelong friendship, everybody can.

One of LaHood's prerogatives when he became the transportation secretary was to revive something known as the Transportation Infrastructure Finance and Innovation Act (TIFIA), which provided low-interest loans for infrastructure projects of "regional or national significance." These loans were designed to kick-start projects and to be used as leverage to raise more investment monies. The act had been passed in 1998, but it had essentially gone dormant, as so many federal acts do. That left, in essence, billions of dollars sitting there with nowhere to go. LaHood wanted to get that money working again, and I wanted to help him do just that, but only in Chicago.

One morning in early 2012, Green, my three-person transportation team, and I left the hotel to go to our meeting with Secretary LaHood and his TIFIA team. Each member of my team—which included Rosie Andolino, who led our aviation department, Forrest Claypool, who ran our city's public transit at the time, and Gabe Klein, our transportation department head—had a homework assignment to bring one bold idea to the LaHood meeting. We went to talk about three things. One was the 95th Street L station on the South Side, presented by Forrest. Another was the O'Hare parking and car rental facility, presented by Rosie. The third came up on the taxi ride over to the meeting. Let's just say that Gabe had forgotten his homework. I was getting very agitated, as we only had seven minutes until we arrived at the transportation department. Just then, the group reminded me that I had read the MacArthur "genius award" winner Jeanne Gang's book on the Chicago waterways and that I had made a campaign pledge about turning Chicago into a two-waterfront city—to fulfill Daniel Burnham's vision. "Let's build a Riverwalk to complement the boathouses you built," they said.

I felt like I'd been struck by lightning. The Chicago River project was one that I had desperately wanted to tackle. My thinking to that point was to wait for exactly the right time. When my cabinet members mentioned it, I realized that the time was now, and that I just needed to figure out how to sell it as a transportation project. The first two projects had video and handout materials. The Riverwalk presentation I would improvise from thin air in the conference room. We had no materials. So let's just say my improv class at Sarah Lawrence came in handy as did my Mediterranean upbringing to talk with my hands.

We met with LaHood to talk about the three possible projects that might qualify for TIFIA loans. Each member of my team presented their idea to LaHood. Of course it was the river project—the idea that was by far our most ambitious and transformative—that he liked the best. It was something that would completely transform the Chicago River, a plan for a walking and biking promenade with boat docks and green spaces that would reopen the river to the city's inhabitants. We called it the Chicago Riverwalk. LaHood looked at me with his forehead furrowed and his eyes squinting: "Rahm, how is this a transportation project?" I looked at him with that look that said, *Are you sitting down?* "Ray, the coast guard and the Army Corps of Engineers manage the river, so it is a natural transportation project." He chuckled and said, "Well, that's pretty good."

LaHood encouraged us to submit applications for the Riverwalk and our other two initiatives. We did, and a year later, in June 2013, we had a $94 million loan from the federal government for the Riverwalk. (Our other two projects—for the revitalization of the 95th Street L station and the rental car facility at O'Hare—would also be funded by TIFIA loans in successive years.) The loan would basically allow us to build the Riverwalk for no local cost. We would pay the money back, with 3.1 percent interest, from revenues generated by tourists who took an architectural boat tour over a thirty-five-year period. We were on our way to finally seeing Daniel Burnham's vision of a two-waterfront city through. "Make no little plans," Burnham once said. "They have no magic to stir men's blood." We took his advice to heart.

———

There's a beautiful quote that I think of often that's been attributed to the Toronto-based architect Ken Greenberg. It's about the rise in the last few decades of urban waterfront parks on repurposed land, which Greenberg has described as "the melting of the industrial glacier."

Our urban waterways, and all the industry and commerce and transportation they supported, were the original drivers in the creation of our world's great cities. We have now returned to those waterways, reimagining and reinventing them. They have formed a bridge from the industrial age to our present age and once again given our cities life and vitality. Our new urban waterfronts are the cornerstones of the revival and resurgence of the city. They help make our cities better places to live, work, and play.

Mikkelsen transformed Copenhagen with the overhaul of the city's former industrial waterfront. Hidalgo has given the Seine back to Parisians. Oslo has a 5.5-mile Harbour Promenade, which links the city to its fjord and is responsible for two brand-new neighborhoods as well as scores of new restaurants and shops. San Antonio was very early to this game with its vibrant Paseo del Rio, which dates back to the 1930s. Washington, D.C., finally put its "other river"—the much-neglected Anacostia—to public use with The Yards, a forty-two-acre development which includes residential, commercial, and office space and a park along the river. The city of Savannah, Georgia, opens up onto River Street. The Three Rivers Heritage Trail in Pittsburgh consists of twenty-four miles of walking and biking paths along that city's famous confluence of rivers. Oklahoma City has a lively entertainment district along its Bricktown Canal.

Brooklyn Bridge Park—built around six former industrial piers along the East River, which have been turned into soccer fields, parks, and basketball courts—is now "the front lawn of Brooklyn," according to Mayor Bill de Blasio. In Seattle, under Mayor Jenny Durkan, the last parts of an elevated highway that once ran through the heart of downtown have been dismantled. In its place the city will construct a twenty-acre park—a true central park for a city that has never had one—that will open up Seattle to its waterfront on the spectacular Puget Sound. In Dallas, former mayor Michael Rawlings began building a $600 million park—all funded by the city—along the Trinity River. At 10,000 acres, this new park will be eleven times larger than New York City's Central Park.

In 2015 we opened the first two parts of the Chicago Riverwalk. Two years later most of it had been completed. The Chicago Riverwalk is 1.25 miles of a continuous promenade in the middle of downtown. It comprises six "rooms," as we call them. There's the Marina (for boat docks), the Cove (for kayaks), the Water Plaza (which has fountains), the Jetty (where you can fish and see floating gardens), the River Theater, and the Boardwalk (which has an accessible walkway and lawn area). There are four boathouses on the North and South Branches from which you can canoe, kayak, or scull, and an outdoor auditorium where we host free public events. It is a beautiful spot, an oasis within an urban setting—it's Chicago's canyon, a river that runs through our amazing architectural landscape. (Others agree: In 2017 the Urban Land Institute gave Chicago its global award for excellence because of the Riverwalk.) The *Financial Times* said of the Riverwalk, "Its success has been instant and electrifying . . . it is an engaging and elegant new platform."

These reinvented waterfronts are more important than they

may seem at first glance. They are an essential part of that trifecta that I've mentioned before, the three things that modern cities must provide in order to thrive: They make a city a better place to live, work, and play. They improve the health of a city and are great for the environment. They enhance aesthetics, nurturing that "city soul," as Mitch Landrieu would call it. They are a huge part of that new urban policy that I've talked about, in the creation of neighborhoods and communities and a city that is connected to itself. Open waterfronts create the connective tissue that binds a city together. And they spur so much economically, from the vendors and tourists and the development that springs up around them.

———

I remember standing on a corner by the Chicago River in 2011 just after I had taken office, at a place called Wolf Point. It was a cold and bleak day, made bleaker by the fact that the area was empty. The area felt old, worn-down, and empty, a forgotten and forbidden part of Chicago.

Things have changed dramatically since, thanks to the Riverwalk and the seeds for growth that it has helped plant. Now at Wolf Point there is a beautiful new waterfront promenade that is vibrant and filled with life. Soon on that very corner where I stood in 2011 there will be a brand-new 813-foot-tall skyscraper that will be occupied by Salesforce, among other companies. Just off the Riverwalk on Wacker Drive, a new 800-foot-tall skyscraper is under construction, and Bank of America has leased 500,000 square feet within it. Also being constructed on the river is the Vista Tower, a joint project of the Magellan Development Group and the Wanda Group. Apple, which is in the process of building twenty new retail stores across the world, put the first of these on the Riverwalk. In all, there are six new office buildings and four new residential buildings under construction on or around the Riverwalk. There are bars and restaurants. Recreation on the river has increased by 66 percent. Vacancies in surrounding buildings dropped from 14 percent in 2017 to 8 percent in 2018. The Riverwalk has created billions' worth of private investment for the city of Chicago. One of my favorite things on the river is a new REI store that encompasses retail and recreation. You can shop there, of course. But you can also rent a kayak to use right there on the river. All of this was done without privatizing the waterfront—there are no billboards or advertisements (except for the ugly sign on the Trump Tower). And we are on schedule to pay back our thirty-five-year TIFIA loan in half that time.

The river has been reborn, and the now two-waterfront city of Chicago has come into its own.

We didn't just stop with the Riverwalk. In 2015 we converted part of the old Meigs Field Airport, on a peninsula in Lake Michigan, into forty acres of parkland, with trails, a lagoon, and wildlife habitat. I also wanted to do something about the congestion on the lake's public space, which is the third most-visited park in the country. But I knew I needed some help. I went to lunch one day with Citadel's Ken Griffin, a bike enthusiast. There I laid out a vision for separate bike and running paths along seventeen miles of the lake. I told him I had $12 million in public funding already secured, but I needed $24 million total. "I need a date," I said.

Four weeks later he texted me. "You've got a date," he said, and pledged to fund the remaining cost. Now our lakefront is safer, less congested, and more pleasurable. In late 2017 we broke ground on a two-mile elevated walking, hiking, running, and biking path along the river that connects the neighborhoods of Irving Park, North Center, Avondale, and Albany Park. The 312 RiverRun (named after a Chicago area code) will have parks, fields, fitness centers, playgrounds, ice-skating rinks, tennis courts, a pool, and some boathouses. Soon the residents of these neighborhoods won't have to take a ten-minute drive to get to open space along the water. It will be right in their backyards. In the spring of 2019 *Outside* magazine rated Chicago as the number one city to live in because of the lakefront and river investments.

Concurrent with this development, we've brought in environmental consultants to help clean up the river and also required that any adjacent buildings must help in the cleanup. Forty years ago there were just seven aquatic species in the Chicago River. Now there are more than fifty-eight. Our goal is to make the river swimmable by 2040. I know that sounds crazy, but I think we'll get there.

The Chicago River now acts as a spine that connects many of the city's neighborhoods. It has stayed true to its transportation roots, connecting Lake Michigan with the heart of the city, except now the transportation is human and it takes place on foot or on a bike. The Chicago River is now very much part of the city and not apart from it.

———

Our green spaces and recreational areas are not just confined to the waterfront, of course. Having open areas within the city, away from the water, is also vitally important.

For decades the residents of the neighborhoods of Bucktown, Wicker Park, Logan Square, and Humboldt Park expressed their desire to transform the old, abandoned elevated Bloomingdale rail line into a walking park, something similar to the High Line in New York City. So we made it happen. The 2.7-mile pedestrian walkway, known now as the 606 (for Chicago's zip code), was started in 2013 and completed just two years later. We accessed something known as the Congestion Mitigation and Air Quality Improvement Program, which is part of the Federal Highway Administration, to pay for nearly half of the 606's $95 million cost. I then leveraged that to get some money from local and state sources and again put on my dancing shoes and went and raised $20 million from corporate and private donations.

On the South Side in Calumet, we reclaimed three hundred acres of an old industrial site and created a nature preserve and the largest dirt bike area in the urban Midwest. In 2017, in addition to the 606, we finished what became known as Chicago Plays!—a five-year, nearly $50 million initiative in which we installed or renovated 362 playgrounds for our kids, including the twenty-acre Maggie Daley Park Playground. During my time as mayor, the city opened 985 acres of parks and 11 miles of new waterfront open space. Now 97 percent of our residents live within a ten-minute walk or less from a park. (Nationally, only 66 percent of the population can say the same.) That will only improve by the end of 2020, when we will have 2,020 acres in total of green and open spaces in Chicago.

Our city is fundamentally changed for the better because of all of this. It is open, accessible, and green and is now a better place than before to live, work, and play.

———

Knox White, the Republican mayor of Greenville, South Carolina, has been in office since 1995 and has transformed his city of 68,543 people since then. He's focused on the downtown area, reviving it by making it walkable and livable. His first move when he took office was to build mixed-use residential buildings, enticing people to move back to the downtown area. Slowly but surely, they came. "There was a time when I knew everyone who lived downtown by name," White says. Retail and commercial buildings and business tenants followed. White was happy with the city's progress: By the dawn of the new millennium, Greenville was well on its way to having a vibrant downtown life, with residents and commerce moving in to live on its beautiful tree-lined streets. One thing kept nagging at him, though, something he believed was holding the city back from its true potential. That was the underutilized Reedy River. "We had a river running through downtown that was basically underdeveloped, and no one went there," he says. "There was a beautiful waterfall on the river, but it had been covered by a highway bridge for forty years. Most people had never seen it."

White wanted to remove the bridge and make the falls area into a park. Initially he faced some opposition to the plan. Some people liked the convenience of driving over the bridge to get to town. More than that, though, most of the citizens of Greenville had no idea what was under the bridge. "So we drew it up for them and showed it to them, the falls, a stunning green space park," he says. "And that began to change minds."

In 2004, Greenville officially opened a stunning renovation of what's known as Falls Park on the Reedy River. "It changed everything," says White. "The wind has been behind our backs ever since." After the park was opened, Greenville lured a minor-league baseball team and built a baseball stadium through a public-private partnership. The city has added another park along the river—the twenty-mile Swamp Rabbit Trail—for hiking and biking. An area of old warehouses and a former public works facility a quarter of a mile upriver from Falls Park is being converted into a sixty-acre park that will have an observation tower, outdoor concert space, playgrounds and "spraygrounds," and open meadows.

Greenville has become a better place to live and play. Because of that, it has attracted employers. Hundreds of millions of dollars of foreign investments have piled into the area. Multinational companies such as BMW, Michelin, and GE have a presence in Greenville now. And that influx of global companies and people has transformed the city even more. It has become more global and more diverse. "We embrace that," White says. "We are unabashedly inclusive. We are part of the world."

That's happened in no small part because of a transformative park in the middle of the city.

———

In the Fallowses' book, *Our Towns,* Deborah Fallows, after visiting countless cities and towns, formulates a theorem: The mark of a successful city is having a riverwalk, even if it doesn't have a river. What she means is that a successful city finds something unique or different about itself—you could call it a personality—and then creates a park or green space around it. "Some cities don't have water," says White. "But every city has something."

Detroit reclaimed part of its downtown from vehicular traffic with the twin parks, Campus Martius (opened in 2004) and Cadillac Square (2007), and $3 billion has since been invested around the perimeters of the parks. Citygarden, a park and sculpture garden in the heart of St. Louis that opened in 2009, offers views of the Gateway Arch. In Birmingham, Alabama, old railroad tracks, once used in the steel industry, were pulled up to create a downtown oasis called Railroad Park. Now a once-blighted area is filled with trees, trails, a lake, and people. Klyde Warren

Park is a 5.2-acre park built in Dallas above a freeway that, until the park opened in 2012, had formed a barrier between the city's Arts District and its downtown.

What these parks do—both those that are on the water and those that are not—is provide a city with a place that's truly for all its citizens. These parks are some of the few places left in the world where people from every walk of life—regardless of race, income, religion—come together and share a common experience. This is especially important at a time when we are all retreating to our self-selected safe spaces. These parks create great financial growth for cities, which is always welcome. But they also provide something that's priceless by unifying a city and helping to create its soul.

———

There is art in the reimagining and revitalization of our old industrial spaces and waterfronts in our cities. There is also art in the funding that makes it happen. In Chicago we tapped the reserves of the federal government for portions of the money. Knox White used public-private partnerships to get Falls Park built. Citygarden and Railroad Park relied on foundations that were created to build them. Funds for Campus Martius and Cadillac Park came from a nonprofit. Klyde Warren Park used a mix of city, state, and federal funds and private donations.

Cities have spurred the ideas and innovations for these transformations and have found creative ways to get the funding. And the best of these ideas have been shared and have spread across the world.

ELEVEN

Horizontal Networks

In the 1960s the city of Paris constructed highways along the banks of the Seine River. The authorities believed the new roads would help alleviate some of the traffic bottlenecks in the inner city. But the opposite occurred. The traffic problems in fact got worse. So did the city's air, choked with the exhaust of some 2,200 cars traveling along the riverbanks per hour. And the highways cut the city and its inhabitants off from one of the most stunning features of Paris: its river.

In the early 2000s a few Parisians came up with a proposal to dismantle one of the highways and turn the southern bank of the river into a vast pedestrian walkway. One of the biggest advocates of this idea was the then–deputy mayor of the city, Anne Hidalgo.

Hidalgo and her cohorts faced a pretty big obstacle: The French government opposed the project. Hidalgo and then-mayor Bertrand Delanoë knew that if the change to the riverbank was going to happen, the city would have to go it alone.

So Delanoë and Hidalgo came up with a plan. It entailed giving the citizens of Paris a small taste of what life might be like without a highway on the Left Bank. They shut down traffic on Sundays and allowed pedestrians to stroll along the river.

The enticement worked: By 2010, Delanoë and Hidalgo had fully drawn plans for a 1.4-mile walkway along the Left Bank, from the Musée d'Orsay to the Alma Bridge, and the support of the public: Parisians voted to fund the project themselves. In 2012, what was known as the Berges de Seine (Banks of the Seine) opened the Left Bank to pedestrians for good.

Two years later, when Hidalgo was elected mayor of Paris, she entered her office with even bigger plans for the Seine. In 2016 the northern bank of the river, too, was "restored," as she says, to pedestrians. The combined riverbank areas—twenty-four-plus acres along more than four miles of river—are now known as the Parc Rives de Seine. The park, which attracts more than one million visitors a year, has returned the river, and in some important way the city, too, to its people.

———

In the summer of 2016, I traveled to Paris to attend the opening of the Right Bank portion of the park. At that point we were just a few months away from opening some of the final sections of the Riverwalk in Chicago, and I was curious to see firsthand the work that had been done in Paris. Hidalgo and I took a long walk along the Right Bank. It was a beautiful sunny summer day, one enhanced by the splendor and serenity of the new walkway along the river. As we were walking and talking, a couple came up to us. "Hi, Mayor Emanuel," they said. "We're from Chicago!"

Hidalgo laughed and joked that I had planted the duo to impress her. I told her that if I'd wanted to impress her, I would have lined up a few dozen people to come say hello. And trust me, that is not beyond me. But the incident got me thinking. This couple from Chicago was visiting Paris—global citizens making connections in global cities. Their home city had been transformed by the rethinking and reinvention of its waterfront. And now they were in Paris, walking along *its* reinvented and transformed waterfront. The Chicago River and the Seine River had defined the histories of their respective cities. Now they were defining the future of those cities—economically, environmentally, recreationally, and culturally.

The respective parks are as distinct and different as their host cities, but they are similar in their beauty and consequence. They had been built around the same time, the ideas—and the coming to fruition of those ideas—happening nearly simultaneously. This was occurring all over the world, these ideas about waterfronts flowing from Greenville to Paris to Chicago to Oslo.

Hidalgo and I talked about this phenomenon. We realized that there had never been a high-profile international meeting of mayors on the topic of the redevelopment of waterfronts in cities and the potential of that to spur economic revivals. So over lunch we agreed that the following March we would cohost one in Chicago.

Seventeen mayors attended, from eleven different countries and five different continents, representing 44 million people in all. Lahore mayor Mubashir Javed came, as did Shenyang vice mayor Huang Kai. Mayor Patricia de Lille flew in from Cape Town. Mayor Lena Malm came from Gothenburg. Haifa mayor Yona Yahav was interested in learning more about conservation ideas for his city's Mediterranean beachfront. Former Mexico City mayor Miguel Mancera was looking for ideas for access to water for his city, which has no natural waterfront. Mayor Michael Rawlings of Dallas came looking for concepts he could use for his Trinity River park. We all shared our ideas openly. I learned a few things from other mayors that I incorporated into the final stages on the eastern end of the Chicago Riverwalk, including some ideas for landscaping and seating.

The waterways meeting in Chicago wasn't sponsored by the United Nations, and we didn't ask permission from the state or commerce department to hold it. It was just us, the mayors from global cities. We just did it. "Through our networks, mayors are the ones who are establishing a strong multilateralism," says Hidalgo. "Our work, on a global scale, promotes and strengthens this multilateralism, which is, in my opinion, the only answer to global governance."

That multilateralism among cities is what Denis Coderre, the former mayor of Montreal (who also attended the waterways conference), calls "urban diplomacy"—the ability of cities, and not nation-states, to work together to find solutions for problems affecting the world. "The best thing is that these problems can be addressed quickly when they are addressed by cities," he says. The world moves fast these days. So do cities. And there is power in the collective way in which they do it. Speed of response is a key factor in the shift of power in the nation-state back to the cities. Cities are adopting a multilateral approach as Trump and other leaders are adopting a unilateral approach. This switch is not a coincidence.

———

Mayors all over the world are doing similar things when it comes to income equality, the climate, infrastructure, and green spaces. There are two reasons for that. The first is that the ideas which are being shared are very good ones. They are solutions to real challenges. They work. Mayors are responsive in real time, or in short order they are gone. The second is that over the last few decades, a new traffic pattern for ideas has evolved and taken shape. Ideas now move around the world horizontally and not vertically, as they once did, from the ground up to national governments. Cities now adopt and adapt ideas and copy and borrow from each other. They also do it with a touch of healthy competitiveness.

Various intermediaries, both formal and informal, help with this horizontal idea-sharing. There is the C40, the Rockefeller Foundation's 100 Resilient Cities, and Bloomberg's various mayor-oriented groups. In America, perhaps the most effective and important group is the U.S. Conference of Mayors, which includes the mayors of cities with a population of 30,000 or more. Though the conference was founded in response to the Great Depression, it has never been more essential than it is now. It acts as a meeting ground for mayors, a place where any and all political labels are shed. There is only the desire to learn from each other and improve. "At the U.S. Conference of Mayors, we love telling each other stories and seeing what everyone is up to," says Pete Buttigieg. "You can learn pretty quickly whether you're ahead or behind the pack."

Tom Tait says organizations like the U.S. Conference of Mayors are a truly *functional* gathering of politicians, a rarity in our political world today. "We all tend to like each other," he says. "Everyone knows we've got issues back at home in our own cities. There's a shared understanding and a camaraderie that comes with that." Says Mitch Landrieu, "Mayors spend a lot of time together. We get to know each other through these gatherings. We love to compare notes and compete with each other. I hated it when someone beat me to something. And I know that feeling was shared."

There are smaller intermediaries, too, that are also effective. Our waterways meeting was an example. So was the meeting for the Chicago Climate Charter. Nan Whaley's Ohio Mayors Alliance is another great example, as is Hidalgo's AIMF (the International Association of Francophone Mayors).

These intermediary organizations, both large and small, can act as the war rooms of urban diplomacy. In 2017, Trump proposed cutting $300 million in funding for the protection of the Great Lakes in his first budget. This meant a lot to me, because one of the first bills I introduced—and passed—as a U.S. congressman was for the restoration of the Great Lakes, something I had worked on with then-president George W. Bush. Trump announced this the day I was hosting the mayors' conference on cities and waterways. So a bunch of us mayors at the conference gave a press conference to go after Trump, what was really one of the first shots across the bow by mayors in this new world where mayors are taking the lead when the federal government is walking away. Our pressure worked. The budget was saved.

Bryan Barnett of Rochester Hills once gathered together twenty-five mayors from southeast Michigan to discuss issues in their area. The most pressing one at the time was the water situation in Flint. Karen Weaver, the mayor of Flint, had just taken office when the crisis hit, so she needed—and got—the help of her fellow mayors. "That's part of the brotherhood and sisterhood that exists among mayors," says Barnett.

Sometimes we just meet each other rather informally, as I did when I traveled to Paris to visit Hidalgo and to see her work on the Seine. I met with Giuseppe Sala of Milan on a few occasions, and we talked about mass transit, waterways, and our 1871 digital start-up center.

During our time together at different gatherings, Mayor Man-

cera and I decided to ramp up our efforts at making Chicago and Mexico City actual sister cities. We went further than just having more direct flights between the cities and meaningless plaques and ceremonies. We actually started creating a business and trade relationship, city to city, not nation to nation. In fact, on my first visit to Mexico City, I pulled up to the city hall and there were protesters in front. I asked Miguel what they were protesting and he told me there had been a change in how the national government granted teacher certification. I said, "I've never felt more at home." I shared many meals with Landrieu and Garcetti where we talked about our respective cities and the issues we faced and how we were planning to tackle them. Khan and I met on numerous occasions, including his first visit to the States, when he made Chicago his first stop after his election.

On that trip we signed a technology partnership, agreeing to share city data with one another. The two of us took a boat tour of the Riverwalk as we discussed his plans for a possible similar park project on the Thames River. And then I took him to a Whole Foods in Chicago's Englewood community to see firsthand the economic spark a grocery store can be in a distressed area. I cannot thank Walter Robb of Whole Foods enough for being willing to bet on Englewood and its residents. And then I took him to my synagogue on the Sabbath. My rabbi stood up and identified Mayor Khan and thanked him for his visit to our synagogue. Then he said he just had one question: "How did you convince Rahm to show up?" To this day Khan teases me about this. I told him I had a sneaking suspicion that his imam would say the same thing. "That's why I've never taken you to my mosque," he said. But in all seriousness, this was an act of symbolism: We are two mayors of different faiths. Our cities work together. Our faiths can work together. Our global cities and residents share many commonalities and share a common destiny. Again, an example of the soft power mayors can exercise, especially at a time of tribal politics.

————

While I was mayor, I shamelessly copied or adopted some of the best ideas of other mayors. When the sixth—and last—section of the Riverwalk was completed, for some reason it did not attract as many people as the other five sections. One day my daughter Ilana and I were in Berlin, on a boat tour of the River Spree. She noticed that the city had put out some Adirondack-style chairs along the riverside, and people really seemed to like them. "Why don't you do that on the last section of the Riverwalk?" she asked. It was a great idea. I asked my people who managed the Riverwalk to get on it. Six weeks later there were still no chairs. I called them again. They said they were still evaluating. "Okay. Stop evaluating now and go to Crate & Barrel and buy forty chairs today," I said. They did, and put them out that afternoon, and people flocked to them immediately, bringing to life the last section of the Riverwalk.

In 2015, Albuquerque started a program for the homeless called There's a Better Way, under then-mayor Richard Berry, a Republican. His city put up signs at intersections that panhandlers were known to frequent, directing them to homeless shelters. It also requisitioned vans to drive to those same spots and offer day-labor jobs—in a landscaping business, for instance—that paid $9 an hour. The city solicited donations from citizens for the homeless, donations that would be far more effective than an on-the-street handout. Giving a panhandler $5 might enable him to get one meal, but a $5 donation to the city's program, with its better pricing for food, could feed as many as twenty people.

We replicated part of this program in Chicago and then went a step further, enacting a tax on Airbnb rentals that raised $3 million for housing for the homeless. (We later put another tax on these rentals to raise money for 150 beds for domestic violence shelters.) We drew inspiration from San Antonio's Paseo del Rio and Hidalgo's work on the Seine for the Riverwalk. The 606 was modeled after the High Line in New York City, just as the idea for our tech center came from Bloomberg's Roosevelt Island center. Replacing all of the streetlights in Chicago with LED lights was an idea I stole from former Vancouver mayor Gregor Robertson. I stole it because it was a very smart idea.

Other ideas have risen nearly simultaneously. Our idea for the Star Scholarship came just as Tennessee was implementing something similar. Greg Fischer in Louisville began to work on his Cradle to Career program around the same time, and Marty Walsh in Boston has since embarked on a similar program. Cities all over the country raised their minimum wages at nearly the same time.

I was also willing to share any of our ideas with anyone who wanted to listen. Or not. Mayor Sylvester Turner of Houston visited us with his team to check out our co-location project, in which we housed libraries within public housing. He's looking into doing the same thing, and so is the city of Brussels. Boston is now in the process of replicating our Becoming a Man mentoring program. Mayor Mike Duggan of Detroit has copied our after-school and summer jobs programs. Mayor Rawlings of Dallas has also copied our Summer of Learning initiative, and while he was here for the waterways conference I picked his brain about Klyde Warren Park and the idea of putting a park above a highway. (Years ago Boston did something like this over its highway tunnel, calling it the "Big Dig.") I wasn't the only one to do this: Atlanta, Philadelphia, Denver, and Los Angeles are also considering the construction of similar parks.

Mayor John Tory of Toronto came to Chicago in 2018, and we visited Maggie Daley and Millennium Parks as well as the River-walk. Tory is interested in doing something similar to the Maggie Daley playground in Toronto but was having trouble getting much traction for the idea in his city council. I offered him some advice: Make it part of some bigger plan for the city. I told him how in order to get Maggie Daley done, I had had to start with a bigger political idea that I knew would have a better chance of success. That political idea was the Chicago Plays! initiative to rebuild 327 playgrounds across the city. Maggie Daley was part of that, and that's how it was built.

There was no federal plan—or federal resources—for any of this. None of these ideas came from the top down, nor did they come from the bottom up, vertically. They spread horizontally. Every mayor has their story of what they've copied and what has been copied from their tenure.

———

These ideas are found all over the place. Imagine for a moment two mayors from the two major political parties in two vastly different parts of the country coming up with the same (winning) idea of running for mayor on the concept of compassion. That happened with Anaheim's Tom Tait (Republican) and Louisville's Greg Fischer (Democrat). "Greg hadn't heard of me and I hadn't heard of him," says Tait.

Fischer also wanted to improve his city through the use of data. Upon taking office, he and his team flew to Baltimore to meet with former mayor Marty O'Malley. "O'Malley had created a city stats process that intrigued us," says Fischer, who would implement some of the lessons he learned from O'Malley into his LouieStat program, which helps the city make decisions based on data. Fischer also wanted to increase his city's innovation processes, so he visited Boston, which has something called the Office of New Urban Mechanics, which encourages new ways of looking at civic innovation in public safety, housing, education, and play and creative spaces. The Bluegrass Economic Advancement Movement (BEAM) agreement between Fischer's Louisville and Mayor Jim Gray's Lexington is groundbreaking, an example of how cities and mayors can work together to enhance a combined area (the two cities are about eighty miles apart). It's not just a political partnership; it's a civic one as well, with the University of Louisville and the University of Kentucky and companies in both cities coming together to create a whole that's much more than the sum of its parts, a superregion that has already become a hub for innovation and advanced manufacturing. The stated goal of BEAM is to "build it locally, sell it globally," and it seeks to add small and medium-sized international exporters to the multinational companies—like Ford, Toyota, and Lockheed Martin—that already have a presence in the region. BEAM has already been an unqualified success, accounting for more than half of the state's record $31 billion in exports on 2017.

Inspiration for ideas comes from many places. Pete Buttigieg brought dockless bike-sharing to the city of South Bend—making it the first city in the world to have the service at scale—in a roundabout manner. He'd first seen the idea of *docked* bike-sharing while on a trip to Copenhagen. "But I didn't think we could afford it because the docking stations were so expensive," he says. Then one day Miro Weinberger, the mayor of Burlington, Vermont, called him. "He told me that he had seen a dockless bike-sharing setup, but he thought that his city, at 40,000 people or so, was too small to utilize it," says Buttigieg. "He wondered if I wanted to take a look at it." (South Bend's population is 102,000.) Buttigieg did, and the stationless service made it workable for South Bend. Buttigieg is also formulating a plan for a high-speed rail service between his city and Chicago, which would cut the commute down to ninety minutes from two hours or more. Like BEAM, this initiative would benefit both cities and an entire area.

Landrieu visited us in Chicago to check out our real-time crime data center, which he replicated in New Orleans's French Quarter. "We've used it at all of our Mardi Gras since then," he says (arrests during the event were cut in half in 2014). Through Bloomberg's What Works Cities, Landrieu says, he learned one of his simplest but most effective lessons. It had to deal with bill collection, a thorn in every mayor's side. "For sewer and water bills, we used to write someone a letter and then another and then another if they didn't pay, and then threaten to shut down their water," he says. Through the Bloomberg group, he learned that London had hit on a more effective idea. "They started sending letters with a different tone," he says. "Something like, 'Dear Mr. Jones: You haven't paid your water bill and we could shut down your water. But we'd like for you to know that 95 percent of the people in your neighborhood are paying their water bills on time and it would really help if you would join them in making sure that our mutual responsibilities are met.' And London's collection rate went up 5 percent after they adopted this new tone in their letters. Sometimes it's just the little-bitty things like that."

There's a lot going on with international mayors. Hidalgo has worked with Mexico City and Medellín on sharing experiences and best practices for urban creativity and civic innovation. She and Khan wrote a joint op-ed about maintaining a close economic and cultural relationship between their cities after Brexit. Khan has met with Ada Colau, the mayor of Barcelona, to discuss housing matters, particularly regarding the delivery of genuinely more affordable homes. In 2016 he hosted a social integration conference that included the mayors of Amsterdam, Athens, and Lisbon, among other cities. "We discussed how cities should respond to the common challenge of ensuring that communities remain integrated and cohesive in a time of rapid change and social upheaval," he says. Khan has also worked closely with other mayors in England. He and Andy Burnham, the mayor of Manchester, have met and discussed the issue of homelessness (or "rough sleeping," as they call it in England). He has also worked with Andy Street, the mayor of the West Midlands, on how to better position the manufacturing industry in that city post-Brexit. "I would rather emulate a good idea from elsewhere than make a bad investment decision," says Khan. "So I'm always looking at what other cities are doing."

Politicians of all stripes—congressmen, governors—share and copy ideas, to be sure. But there are some differences when it comes to mayors: The sharing is done mostly in a nonpartisan way, and the ideas can be implemented with alacrity. Garcetti says this sharing and copying "is what makes mayors special." He talks about a dinner he hosted at a U.S. Conference of Mayors meeting a few years ago in Boston. The dinner had no speeches and no agenda. It was just twenty-five mayors sitting together and dining and talking. "I remember John Cranley, the Democratic mayor of Cincinnati, talking to Tomás Regalado, the Republican mayor of Miami, all night long," says Garcetti. "They were talking about immigration and climate change, and only at the end of the night did they mention their political parties. These were guys who were interested in city and country and solutions first. Both had positions that could be seen as progressive, both pro-immigrant, -infrastructure, -environment. You can't just ignore these problems. They don't just magically go away. As Mayor Pete Buttigieg once said, you can't say you've fixed a pothole if you haven't. People will call BS."

To further all of the momentum and initiative going on in the new global cities, in 2015 I asked the Chicago Council of Foreign Affairs to create a global cities conference, which Tom and Margot Pritzker and the *Financial Times* have underwritten. For five consecutive years the council has hosted mayors from around the globe in Chicago to discuss initiatives and solutions to command challenges.

———

There was a time in our nation's—and the world's—history when ideas moved more vertically. The bones of the New Deal— from worker's compensation to the workweek to the minimum wage—were all fleshed out in states like New York and Wisconsin. More recently, the health-care plan that Mitt Romney devised while he was governor of Massachusetts turned out to be a road map for the Affordable Care Act. The best ideas rose to the top and were spread around from there.

The best ideas today, however, usually hit a ceiling on the way up and never reach the top. Ideas are now shared under that ceiling. There is no national plan. It's all left up to mayors and their cities and the various entities that inhabit those cities: the universities, nonprofits, foundations, private sector, and citizens.

Again, look at free community college. There's been no impetus at the federal level to do anything to advance this educational innovation. In fact, while cities and states are making progress on cost-free higher education, Washington is having another year of endless debate about college costs, and doing nothing about it.

The horizontal movement of ideas is a new phenomenon. Despite the power of our federal government and all of the attention that it receives, much of the governmental power in the United States is diffused. A lot of it lies in the hands of our cities. Cities have chosen openness and a willingness to share ideas, enacting progressive, forward-thinking initiatives. And that's not the case just in this country. It's the same all over the world. "The multilateralism of city diplomacy brings solutions to the issues we all are facing today, when the nation-state's diplomacy is being adversely affected by isolationism," says Hidalgo.

Philip Zelikow has written about how lonely it can feel for cities and mayors who are innovating and solving problems, how embattled they can feel in the face of a national government that provides so little help and support. He says that these lonely voices "don't yet realize there's a common melody." James Fallows, too, has written about this, about how "the people who have been reweaving the national fabric will be more effective if they realize how many other people are working toward the same end."

I think we're here now. I think with the rate and speed with which mayors and cities are sharing their experiences, rejecting isolationism and working together to create a new form of political power, there is now a realization of a common melody. The power of that common melody will someday be too strong for our nation-states to ignore. My belief is that the horizontal spreading of ideas will eventually rise like a great tide, and the best of those ideas will eventually reach our national governments, where they will be even more effectively spread and more helpful to the people of the world. Until then, mayors and local government are seizing ever more power into their own hands.

TWELVE

The Future

There is, of course, such a thing as a bad mayor. There are the obvious examples. You may remember Rob Ford, the crack-smoking former mayor of Toronto. The crack was just one of many scandals. Ford's great sin when it came to his constituents was that his scandals made everything about him and not about his city. Kwame Kilpatrick, the former mayor of Detroit, was charged in 2008 with ten felony counts and was eventually convicted—and jailed—for perjury and obstruction of justice. Kilpatrick spent his mayoral tenure looking after himself and not his city. Billy Wilson, the former mayor of Greenbrier, Tennessee, was charged with stealing $60,000 from a Toys for Tots campaign in 2013. He resigned the following year and somehow escaped a jail sentence (though he was forced to pay back the money). In 2018, Ben Zahn, the mayor of Kenner, Louisiana, banned his parks and recreation department from buying Nike products after that company aired a commercial featuring Colin Kaepernick, the NFL quarterback who famously kneeled during the national anthem to protest racial injustice in the U.S. When Zahn's attempted ban was revealed, it divided his city. Many citizens of Kenner took to the streets to protest, joined by some members of the New Orleans Saints. Only after the harsh blowback—and after talking to an attorney—did Zahn rescind the ban. Then, too, a good rule of thumb is this: Don't sell your children's books to entities that do business with your city, as Baltimore mayor Catherine Pugh did.

Scandals, corruption, and wading too far into national issues are certainly signs of bad mayors. But some of the attributes of a bad mayor are more subtle. A bad mayor is one who views their job as just making sure the proverbial (or in some cases literal) trains run on time. This technical work is something every mayor has to do, of course, just as every NFL quarterback must be able to take the snap from the center. But that's merely the beginning of the job. Bad mayors don't stretch themselves, don't address challenges, lose their nerve, deny that the challenges exist. I've seen these mayors. We all have. They can at times even win reelection. But they are still failing. One measure of a good mayor is how long you've served. Another measure is what you accomplished while you served. A failed mayor is one who doesn't honestly confront problems and reach out and hold the hands of the public as they march down the road of change.

———

When I took office, Chicago had the shortest school day of any major city in America. We were the only big city that failed to provide full-day kindergarten. Our high school graduation rate was one of the lowest in America for a major city, and we did not even record college acceptance rates. In the 1980s, former secretary of education William Bennett cited Chicago as the worst school system in America. Today, the nationally recognized expert from Stanford Sean Reardon cites the Chicago academic growth rate as higher than 96 percent of all school districts in the United States. Also, among the one hundred largest school districts in the country, Chicago has the highest academic growth rate between the third- and eighth-grade level. When you think of all the challenges and all the possibilities a mayor faces, the ability to make this impactful a change is what makes the work so rewarding. To achieve these successes, we have to confront our shortcomings head on.

Change is our new constant. It comes swiftly, unannounced. And the hardest thing to figure out is how to make change a friend and not a foe. A mayor who denies change is going to fail. He will fail in his responsibility to the public to better prepare his city for the future. When I closed forty-nine failing schools as part of our reform of the Chicago public school system, it was very unpopular politically. But it had to be done, for the future of those students who were trapped in those schools, and because we desperately need to be preparing our eight-year-olds for the information economy, in order to give them a brighter future. More important, and of equal political value, when it came to fighting Springfield for equitable funding, the willingness to clean up our own fiscal issues gave the city the ability to make a strong case, and to dismiss all those who for decades had derailed equitable funding as a Chicago bailout. In that fight we implemented a political strategy of being in the boat with all other cities with predominantly low-income children, rather than on a raft by ourselves. This enabled us to defeat Governor Rauner in his attempt to label the funding a Chicago bailout, and to make him sign the new funding formula that brings 425 million more dollars to Chicago's students. Mitch Landrieu took on his firefighters' union. Jim Brainard installed more than a hundred roundabouts in his city to slow down traffic, ease congestion, and fight pollution. Garcetti and I pushed through significant renovations of our airports. Pete Buttigieg gave his city employees paid family leave. Knox White knocked down a highway bridge to create a new downtown with a waterfall park. Change always comes. Act on it. Bad mayors mimic their federal government counterparts. Denial is not a long-term strategy in local government. Unfortunately, it is in national ones.

A bad mayor doesn't use the bully pulpit to positive affect. "It is an underused thing," says Tom Tait. "But mayors can, and should, affect culture for the better. It can take a long time and you have to be persistent, but it changes everything." A bad mayor doesn't use his or her position to lead, to convene, to cajole. Remember what Greg Fischer said: "Citizenship is a participation sport." A bad mayor asks nothing of his or her citizens, universities, businesses, religious institutions, or nonprofits when it comes to helping make the city work and get better.

There is also such a thing as a bad or failing city, and it has mostly to do with livability. Nine out of the ten most polluted cities in the world are in India, according to the World Health Organization. *The New York Times* reported in early 2019 that the inhabitants of these cities were showing up in emergency rooms unable to breathe, and that kids were vomiting in schools because of the air quality. In 2017 a collective 1.24 million people died as a result of pollution in these cities. India's cities are not alone. In Beijing, the 5 million automobiles and coal-burning and construction dust have made that Chinese city one of the most polluted in the world. In addition, 40 percent of Beijing's water supply is too polluted to use thanks to chemical discharges from industry. Shanghai is unable to use 56 percent of its water supply because of pollution. Pollution problems in the United

States are not nearly as profound as they are in some of these cities in the Far East, but they do exist. In Brady, Texas, the drinking water was found to have nine times the acceptable level of radium in 2018. Flint, Newark, and Pittsburgh have been battling lead problems in their drinking water for years.

The Indian cities have taken a small step recently to address their air pollution by setting up monitoring sites and collecting data. Leaders in Beijing came to Chicago in 2018 to study our parks system, with the hope of creating more green spaces in their city to help the quality of life. Brady is seeking a federal grant to replace its water system. Both Flint and Pittsburgh are actively addressing their water problems.

These are all positive steps. But much more will have to be done. The inhabitants of these cities will demand it. *The New York Times* reported that corporations are now refusing to move to the polluted cities in India. Most certainly those who are able to move out of those cities are already doing so. If polluted cities don't literally clean up their act, they will wither.

The modern city under the modern mayor must become a place where people can live, work, and play. Finding the equilibrium among those three needs determines a city's viability, today and into the future.

But no city has yet found the perfect balance. Even good, healthy cities have serious problems that can seem intractable. As I have mentioned, the rate of gun violence in Chicago, though steadily getting better, is still a tragedy and still needs a lot of work. Even though New York City mayor Bill de Blasio is not in charge of his city's mass transit system (the governor of New York is), he can't just punt the problems currently plaguing the system upstairs. He has to do whatever it takes to make sure that the subway system is modernized. If he doesn't, the progress of his great city will come to a halt, and the city will choke under his watch. In San Francisco, as the technology sector thrives, so, unfortunately, does rampant homelessness.

The latter problem is a symptom of what I believe is one of the biggest challenges that face cities now and will face them in the future. That problem is the real cost of urban prosperity. One of the prime drivers behind the homelessness problem in San Francisco, and many other cities for that matter, is the rise in the cost of rent and the lack of affordable housing. These factors have not only created more homeless people. They have begun pushing out the middle class, which is choosing to live elsewhere (this is one of the reasons that Google and Salesforce and other big tech companies have been opening new campuses in Chicago and other cities). If we're not careful, what we are left with in these cities with unaffordable rent and housing problems is a very rich upper class and a very poor lower class, with no one in between and no bridge on which to traverse that gap.

Gentrification is a serious issue. It is a little secret that no one talks about much when it comes to the dropping rates of crime in our cities. Yes, the revival and reclamation of downtowns and neighborhoods and better policing and better data and general prosperity have been the main drivers in the drop in crime. But gentrification—filling formerly impoverished neighborhoods with more affluent residents—has also played a role. However, the displacement that comes with gentrification is a big problem. New York's High Line has caused higher rental rates in its surrounding neighborhood, pushing out people and businesses and restaurants that had been there for decades. We have faced the same issue with the 606. One of the neighborhoods the walkway runs through is Humboldt Park, a Puerto Rican enclave. After the 606 was built, median house prices in the neighborhood rose 45 percent. The neighborhood is now being populated by young, fairly well-off residents with college degrees. The former residents, some of whose families had been there for generations, are being pried out. A similar change is happening in Ukrainian Village and Pilsen, two Chicago neighborhoods.

The challenge mayors face is to create and foster the economic engine that is development, but to do so without rampant displacement. We've tried what I call "managed gentrification" or "development without displacement" in some Chicago neighborhoods, such as Pilsen, providing assistance on mortgages for residents and making sure we keep some affordable housing in the mix. The results thus far, though, have been far from perfect. I have studied this problem for decades now, and I have yet to see an effective policy. But it's essential that all mayors continue that search and try new approaches until a suitable answer is found. In the end, the solution will be a combination of zoning reforms, new housing with additional affordability goals, tax incentives, tax relief, and mixed use and co-locations with community benefits.

Another one of the big stumbling blocks in American cities is the severe rise in the costs of pensions. The fact that U.S. cities are now approaching $4 trillion in pension debt is a big flashing yellow light for cities that this could become a full-blown crisis. We have to find a way for retired city workers to get their pensions without having the payments on the pensions break a city's back. Cities are the last remaining places in the U.S. where progressive politics exist, where programs that actually help people are implemented. Huge burdensome pension payments and health-care costs, which only divide the pie and don't grow it, run the risk of stunting those progressive policies and investments. The burden of paying for pensions—or sometimes paying for just the interest on the pensions—can become such that there is no money left over for new libraries, early childhood education, infrastructure improvement, climate change initiatives, mass transit. For cities, it becomes a choice between paying 3 percent compounded interest for someone who retired at age fifty-five and paying the salary of a bright young teacher who has the potential to change many lives for the better. We must continue to pay pensions, of course. Those workers earned it. So what do we do?

Sylvester Turner in Houston worked with his state legislature to rein in the costs of his city's pensions. He started with his city employees, crafting a rational plan that asked for sacrifices from them and the city. He then took that plan to the state legislature and cajoled and pleaded with them until they did what was right. All mayors will have to take a look at what Sylvester did to see if it's feasible for their cities. The result in Houston is not perfect, but it's a significant step in the right direction. Because there is a middle ground, a reasonable space, that we can all find here. We have to.

I swore after I left the Obama administration that I would never deal with health care again. But I had to. When I took office in Chicago, our health-care costs were the third-biggest item in the budget, and they were growing at an unhealthy clip of 10 percent a year. I worked on a wellness plan for our employees (which dramatically improved health), and renegotiated better contracts than those that are known as the Olympic contracts with the labor unions and retirees. After ten years of no changes, we were able to secure increases in the copays, change the deductibles, alter prescription drug coverage, and narrow hospital networks for nearly all forty-two labor agreements. Combining these changes with other initiatives, we were able to control health-care costs. The result: When I left office, the health-care costs for the city were 7 percent lower than projected before I became mayor. If other cities do not do something similar, they will find themselves in the same predicament that the federal government is in. Today our federal government is a defense budget that also pays Social Security, Medicare, and Medicaid. If cities are not careful, they, too, could become a public safety budget that pays pension and health-care costs, crowding out all investments in education, libraries, parks, and transportation. The national debt is currently 78 percent of the national income. It is projected to reach 100 percent in the next ten years and 200 percent by 2050. A primary reason for the skyrocketing debt: Social Security and Medicare, which are in effect our national pension plans. It's projected that these two programs will run a cash deficit of *trillions* in the next thirty years. Cities must find a way to avoid falling into a similar debt trap, and they will have to do it quickly. I want to be clear: Social Security and Medicare are not the problem. They reflect a deeper problem embedded in our tax policies. (Another big issue when it comes to federal government funding gaps is, of course, our grossly unfair and regressive tax system, which greatly favors the wealthy and penalizes the middle class. It also starves all other investments.)

All of this—the costs of urban prosperity and the pension debts—is tied to that single biggest issue for mayors and cities that I wrote about earlier: combating income inequality. Affordable housing is a key to narrowing the income gap. Ensuring that cities have the money to spend on access to education (at all levels, from pre-K to college) and teachers and quality of life and finding the balance among live, work, and play—not just shoveling money into the bottomless chasms of legacy costs—is also key. It's all about providing equitable access to the new global economy. If we don't figure these things out, our cities may become smaller versions of our ineffective and broken federal government.

If not handled swiftly and well, these three interrelated issues—the costs of urban prosperity, soaring pensions, and income equality—threaten to undo all of the great progress made in our cities.

———

This is all so vitally important because the future of progressive politics lies with our mayors and not our national governments. This is a shift that many in the Democratic Party haven't caught up with yet. They still turn their eyes to the federal government, looking for salvation, because we are all correctly enamored with the New Deal, the Fair Deal, the New Frontier, and the Great Society. But the evidence is already there for all to see. The federal government has long been bereft of the true two-party compromise that created progressive progress. This situation has only gotten worse under Trump. The federal judiciary is now stacked against progressives, from Trump's two Supreme Court placements to the countless federal judge appointments that have been ushered through the Senate by Majority Leader Mitch McConnell. Any hope of turning this tide starts locally, in our cities, where progressive politics can—and do—flourish. The future of the Democratic Party to some extent lies locally.

Speaking of the Senate, do not look to that body to become a beacon of progressive action anytime soon. In fact, it is already a prime example of the dysfunction in our federal government, and it will only be getting worse. The Senate was originally structured to create a balance between densely and sparsely populated states. It has now become grossly imbalanced, and the prospect of finding any equilibrium does not look good. "By 2040 or so, 70 percent of Americans will live in fifteen states. Meaning 30 percent [of voters] will choose seventy senators," wrote Norman Ornstein of the American Enterprise Institute. "And the 30 percent will be older, whiter, more rural, more male than the 70 percent." This, he points out, is "wholly unrepresentative of the diversity in the country and an immense challenge to the legitimacy of our system." And according to Ornstein, when it comes to our Electoral College system, things are no better. He has pointed out that an individual voter in, say, Wyoming, has more than triple the weight in electoral votes of an individual voter in California.

Traditionally, progressives have been the party of the federal government. This goes back to the New Deal, the Civil Rights Act, and the Great Society. The federal government still has the ability to do good work for its constituents, and hopefully one day it will again. What it lacks is the willpower. It's no longer a progressive entity. It would behoove progressives now, given their dominance in urban areas, to concentrate on local government, not to think of policies going from top down or bottom up but instead to think of them as flowing horizontally, across the country and across the world, from city to city to city.

This development is not something to fear. It is that change I talked about. It is here now and it is the future. There will be one hundred or so great cities that will lead the world. They will look a bit like city-states. They will be smart and safe and diverse and environmentally aware and economically healthy. They will influence the world and national governments with gathering strength. None of the three city-states that exist now—Vatican City, Monaco, and Singapore—quite fits the bill. Vatican City is a one-religion theocracy; Monaco lacks diversity and functions mainly as a tax haven for the rich; Singapore has many good traits—diversity, a strong economy, a healthy city—but its authoritarian bent cannot be ignored.

There are the nascent city-states of Hamburg, Berlin, and Bremen, which have representation in the national legislature and the ability to initiate legislation. In Denmark, too, cities already negotiate with the national government on annual budgets.

But what I'm talking about here is less formal. And it is already happening. The nation city, if you will, that has already emerged, that drives the economic, cultural, and intellectual energy of the world. That innovates. That addresses real challenges in real time. That works.

———

In their book, *The New Localism,* Bruce Katz and Jeremy Nowak talk about the hopefulness they feel about the innovations, ideas, and general competency of local governments. James and Deborah Fallows find much of the same positivity in the high functioning of local governments in their book, *Our Towns.* I am optimistic, too. That "common melody" that Philip Zelikow talks about is gaining in voice and volume, getting louder and louder with each passing moment. It is a very good thing that there is a part of government—and one that so closely touches our lives—that *is* working. The best of the innovations and ideas now being generated and implemented and shared and road-tested within cities will reach the people of the world. They already are. This is the nation city.

Our hope lies with our mayors. They make the world work. They have provided a necessary counterbalance to some of the failures of our national governments. They work together—regardless of political party or national origin or city size—and share ideas and get things done, reaching the same ends with different means, if that's what it takes. The best of them make their cities better places to live, work, and play. With the help of universities and nonprofits, they can create—and then scale— vitally important programs like BAM and the Star Scholarship. I'm full of hope because of what mayors have been able to accomplish, individually and collectively, when it comes to addressing the world's most pressing problems.

Bryan Barnett of Rochester Hills is optimistic, too: "Mayors have earned trust, and we're given the liberty to try and bring solutions to communities because of that trust. That's a very productive thing."

So is Louisville's Greg Fischer: "A lot of it is about increasing our mind frame about what's possible when it comes to providing a brighter future for everyone. I'm confident we are getting there."

So is Nan Whaley: "Mayors are on the ground and we have to be pragmatic. We can move quickly and transform things very fast. The future is better because of that."

Income inequality, the environment, immigration, housing, education, infrastructure, mounting pension debt, the costs of prosperity—all of these issues confront mayors and cities, and they require constant work and vigilance. These issues are all intertwined. They're about making the world work and making it a better place. It is our mayors who stand on the front line when it comes to these issues, confronted by "the fierce urgency of now," as Martin Luther King, Jr., once said.

Our cities are our places of opportunity. They were for my grandfather. They are for me. For you. For everyone in the world.

They contain all the peril in today's world.

More important, they also contain all of the promise.

Acknowledgments

To Presidents Clinton and Obama, I thank you for your tireless service to this great country, and for the opportunities you gave me to help in that service.

To the people of the great city of Chicago, I thank you for the trust you demonstrated in me, and I am exceedingly proud of all that we accomplished together.

To my City Hall staff and cabinet, I thank you for your dedication to public service, and for your sacrifice on behalf of our great city. And to my friends and supporters who were a bulwark for me during my time in public office, specifically Michael Sacks, David Axelrod, Bruce Reed, and Paul Begala, thank you for always being there.

To my agents at William Morris Endeavor and the good folks at Alfred A. Knopf, I thank you for helping make this project come to life.

To my parents and my two brothers, thank you for helping me find my voice and my calling in public service. Finally, to Amy, Zachariah, Ilana, and Leah, I thank you for everything, for sacrificing and allowing me to do what I love to do. I love you.

Selected Bibliography

Barber, Benjamin. *If Mayors Ruled the World: Dysfunctional Nations, Rising Cities.* Yale University Press. New Haven and London. 2013.

Emanuel, Ezekiel J. *Brothers Emanuel: A Memoir of an American Family.* Random House. New York. 2013.

Fallows, Deborah, and James Fallows. *Our Towns: A 100,000-Mile Journey into the Heart of America.* Pantheon. New York. 2018.

Glaeser, Edward. *Triumph of the City: How Our Greatest Invention Makes Us Richer, Smarter, Greener, Healthier, and Happier.* Penguin. New York. 2011.

Jacobs, Jane. *The Death and Life of Great American Cities.* Random House. New York. 1961.

Katz, Bruce, and Jeremy Nowak. *The New Localism: How Cities Can Thrive in the Age of Populism.* Brookings Institution Press. Washington, D.C. 2018.

Quinones, Sam. *Dreamland: The True Tale of America's Opiate Epidemic.* Bloomsbury. New York. 2015.

Sharkey, Patrick. *Uneasy Peace: The Great Crime Decline, the Renewal of City Life, and the Next War on Violence.* Norton. New York. 2019.

Steuerle, C. Eugene. *Dead Men Ruling: How to Restore Fiscal Freedom and Rescue Our Future.* Century Foundation Press. New York. 2014.

Rahm Emanuel was the mayor of the city of Chicago from 2011 to 2019. Prior to becoming mayor, Emanuel served as the White House chief of staff to President Barack Obama and served three terms in the U.S. House of Representatives representing Chicago's Fifth District. He previously served as a key member of the administration of President Bill Clinton from 1993 to 1998, rising to serve as senior adviser to the president for policy and strategy.

Emanuel graduated from Sarah Lawrence College in 1981 and received a master's degree in speech and communications from Northwestern University in 1985. He is married to Amy Rule, and they have three children.

A NOTE ON THE TYPE

This book was set in Minion, a typeface produced by the Adobe Corporation specifically for the Macintosh personal computer and released in 1990. Designed by Robert Slimbach, Minion combines the classic characteristics of old-style faces with the full complement of weights required for modern typesetting.

Typeset by Scribe,
Philadelphia, Pennsylvania

Printed and bound by Berryville Graphics,
Berryville, Virginia

Designed by Cassandra J. Pappas